WoRd STREtChers

Vocabulary activities to develop
and extend word mastery skills

John Flatt

Name: _____

How many words can you spot around this circle?

1 Start anywhere and move around the circle in a clockwise direction, for example *her*.

2 All words must be made up of consecutive letters.

3 Write any words you find on the pad.

4 If you're not sure of a word's spelling or meaning, check it in your dictionary.

5 Try to make your own 20-letter circle with 25 words hidden around it.

6 Colour in this activity page and give yourself the award if you deserve it.

W H E R E
M E
O D
S O
N E
R V
A E
E Y R

Target: 15 words

1st

1

Name: _____

How many words can you spot around this circle?

1   Start anywhere and move around the circle in a clockwise direction, for example *top*.

2   All words must be made up of consecutive letters

3   Write any words you find on the pad.

4   If you're not sure of a word's spelling or meaning, check it in your dictionary.

5   Try to make your own 20-letter circle with 15 words hidden around it.

6   Colour in this activity page and give yourself the award if you deserve it.

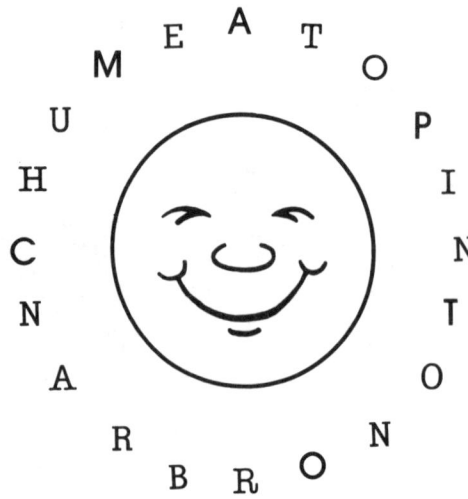

M E A T O
U   P
H   I
C   N
N   T
A   O
R   N
B R O

Target: 15 words

WoRd STRetchers

CIRCLE SPOTTERS

ACTIVITY SHEET 2

1st

Name: _____

How many words can you spot around this circle?

1 Start anywhere and move around the circle in a clockwise direction, for example *you*.

2 All words must be made up of consecutive letters

3 Write any words you find on the pad.

4 If you're not sure of a word's spelling or meaning, check it in your dictionary.

5 Try to make your own 20-letter circle with 25 words hidden around it.

6 Colour in this activity page and give yourself the award if you deserve it.

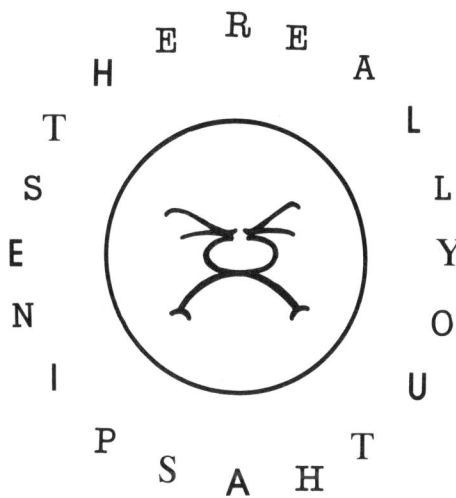

Target: 20 words

CIRCLE SPOTTERS

ACTIVITY SHEET 3

3

Name: _____

How many words can you spot around this circle?

1 Start anywhere and move around the circle in a clockwise direction, for example *net*.

2 All words must be made up of consecutive letters

3 Write any words you find on the pad.

4 If you're not sure of a word's spelling or meaning, check it in your dictionary.

5 Try to make your own 20-letter circle with 25 words hidden around it.

6 Colour in this activity page and give yourself the award if you deserve it.

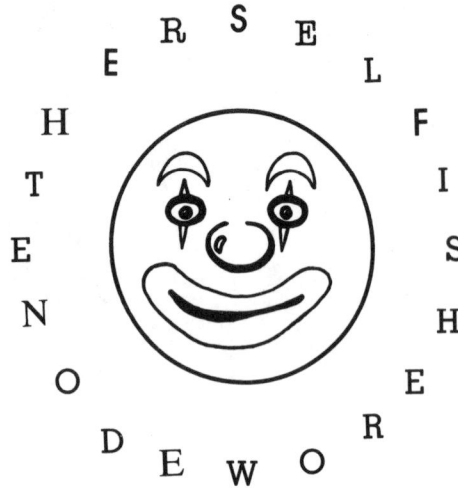

Target: 20 words

WoRd STRetchers

CIRCLE SPOTTERS
ACTIVITY SHEET 4

Name: _____

What sort of a magician are you? How many different words can you find in this 3 × 3 grid?

1 Make as many different words as you can from the letters in the grid. List the words on the lines below.

2 A letter cannot be used more than once in any of your words, unless it is repeated in the grid.

3 Letters may be reused in different words.

4 If you're not sure of a word's spelling or meaning, check it in your dictionary.

5 Colour the activity sheet and enter the number of words you found on the 'Word Wizard' certificate.

e	t	m
z	e	b
w	a	r

WORD WIZARD AWARD

_____

_____

_____

_____

_____

_____

_____

_____

Name: _____

What sort of a magician are you? How many different words can you find in this 3 × 3 grid?

1 Make as many different words as you can from the letters in the grid. List the words on the lines below.

2 A letter cannot be used more than once in any of your words, unless it is repeated in the grid.

3 Letters may be reused in different words.

4 If you're not sure of a word's spelling or meaning, check it in your dictionary.

5 Colour the activity sheet and enter the number of words you found on the 'Word Wizard' certificate.

w	f	t
o	e	s
h	o	n

WORD WIZARD AWARD

_____

_____

_____

_____

_____

_____

_____

_____

_____

WORD MYSTERIES TO MARVEL OVER...

Name: _____

What sort of a magician are you? How many different words can you find in this 3 × 3 grid?

1 Make as many different words as you can from the letters in the grid. List the words on the lines below.

2 A letter cannot be used more than once in any of your words, unless it is repeated in the grid.

3 Letters may be reused in different words.

4 If you're not sure of a word's spelling or meaning, check it in your dictionary.

5 Colour the activity sheet and enter the number of words you found on the 'Word Wizard' certificate.

h	i	c
e	x	s
y	l	d

WORD STRETCHERS

'TIS MAGIC ACTIVITY SHEET 3

WORD WIZARD AWARD

WORD MYSTERIES TO MARVEL OVER...

Name: ______________________

Word Stretchers

’TIS MAGIC

ACTIVITY SHEET 4

What sort of a magician are you? How many different words can you find in this 3 × 3 grid?

1 Make as many different words as you can from the letters in the grid. List the words on the lines below.

2 A letter cannot be used more than once in any of your words, unless it is repeated in the grid.

3 Letters may be reused in different words.

4 If you're not sure of a word's spelling or meaning, check it in your dictionary.

5 Colour the activity sheet and enter the number of words you found on the 'Word Wizard' certificate.

e	g	h
a	t	p
r	v	u

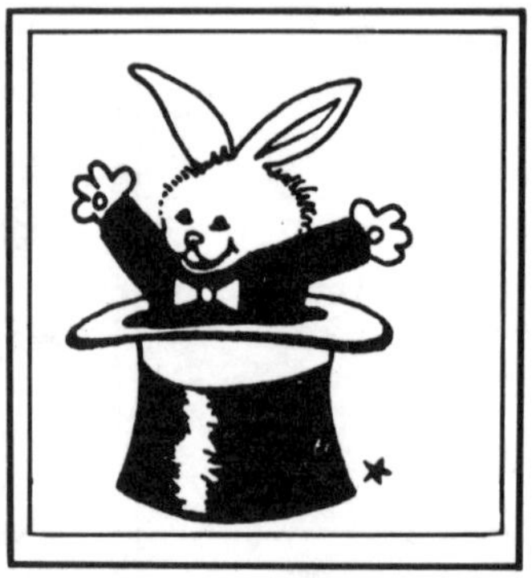

WORD WIZARD AWARD

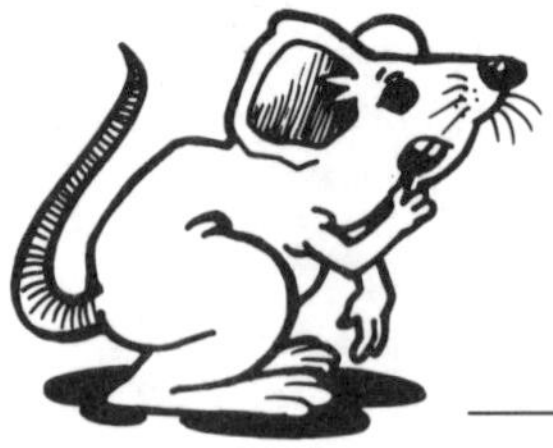

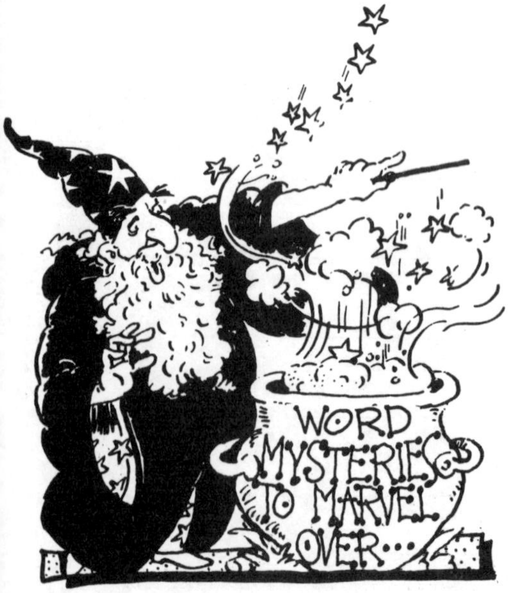

Name: _____

On each key below is a keyword. Using only the letters found in each keyword, how many different words can you find?

1 Make as many different words as you can from the letters on one of the keys. List these words on the pad provided.

2 Do the same for each of the other keywords.

3 A letter cannot be used more than once in any of your words, unless it is repeated in the keyword.

4 Letters may be reused in different words.

Colour the activity sheet and the number of locks you can open.

- For finding 20 words, colour in one lock

- For finding 30 words, colour in two locks

- For finding 40 words, colour in three locks

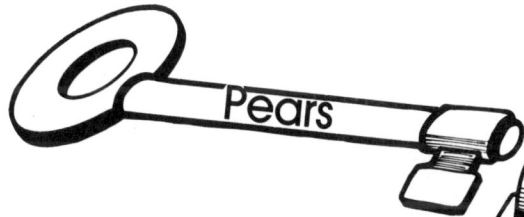

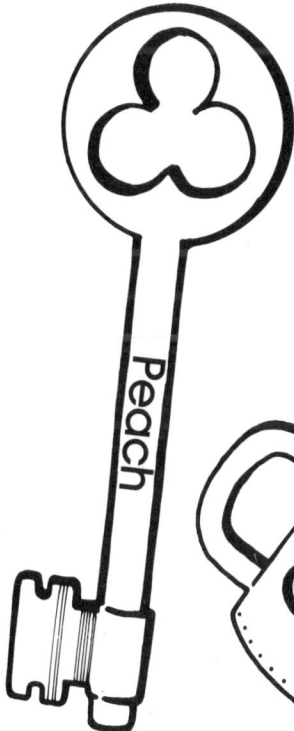

Name: _____

On each key below is a keyword. Using only the letters found in each keyword, how many different words can you find?

1   Make as many different words as you can from the letters on one of the keys. List these words on the pad provided.

2   Do the same for each of the other keywords.

3   A letter cannot be used more than once in any of your words, unless it is repeated in the keyword.

4   Letters may be reused in different words.

Colour the activity sheet and the number of locks you can open.

- For finding 20 words, colour in one lock

- For finding 30 words, colour in two locks

- For finding 40 words, colour in three locks

WoRd STRetchers

KEY WORDS ACTIVITY SHEET 2

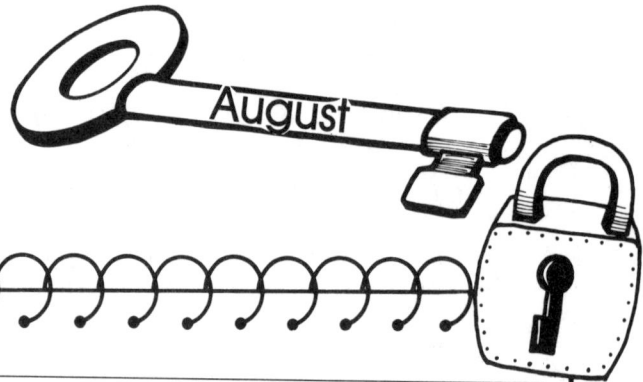

Name: _____

On each key below is a keyword. Using only the letters found in each keyword, how many different words can you find?

1 Make as many different words as you can from the letters on one of the keys. List these words on the pad provided.

2 Do the same for each of the other keywords.

3 A letter cannot be used more than once in any of your words, unless it is repeated in the keyword.

4 Letters may be reused in different words.

Colour the activity sheet and the number of locks you can open.

- For finding 20 words, colour in one lock

- For finding 30 words, colour in two locks

- For finding 40 words, colour in three locks

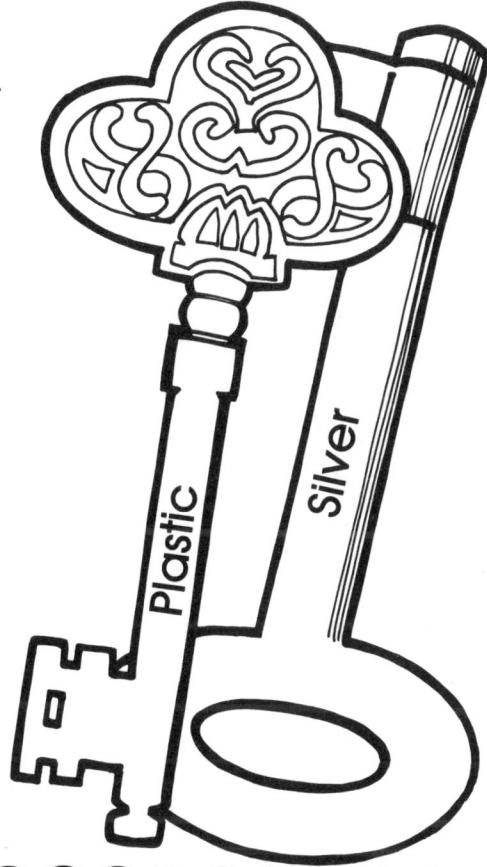

WoRd STRetchers

KEY
WORDS
ACTIVITY
SHEET 3

11

Name: _____

On each key below is a keyword. Using only the letters found in each keyword, how many different words can you find?

1 Make as many different words as you can from the letters on one of the keys. List these words on the pad provided.

2 Do the same for each of the other keywords.

3 A letter cannot be used more than once in any of your words, unless it is repeated in the keyword.

4 Letters may be reused in different words.

Colour the activity sheet and the number of locks you can open.

- For finding 20 words, colour in one lock

- For finding 30 words, colour in two locks

- For finding 40 words, colour in three locks

WoRd STRetchers

KEY
WORDS
ACTIVITY
SHEET 4

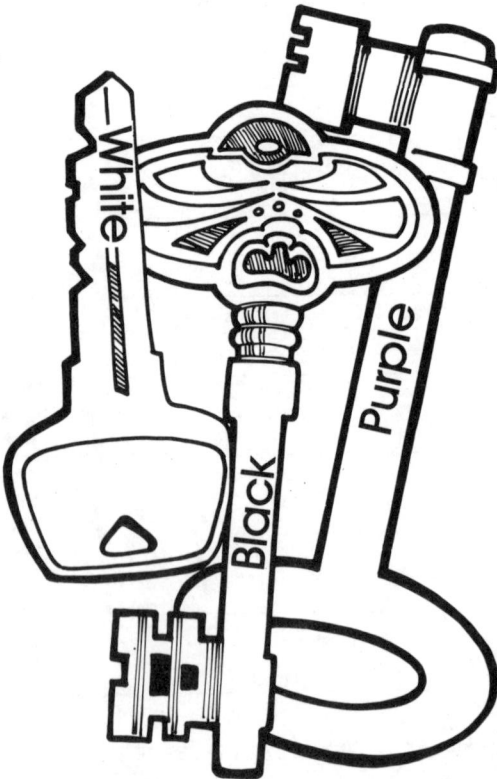

Yellow

Crimson

White

Purple

Black

Name: _____

**Find anagrams for these words and see if you can fly
your rocket back to Earth.**

1 Look at the letters in each word.
2 Rearrange all of the letters to
  form a new word. This is an
  'anagram'.
3 Write the anagram in the space
  provided.
4 For each correct anagram colour
  in one of the sections in the
  rocket's trail.
5 If all your answers were correct,
  you should get back to Earth with
  fuel to spare.

on _____

now _____

eat _____

tac _____

star _____

pets _____

from _____

pool _____

lamp _____

meat _____

leap _____

keen _____

melon _____

ought _____

broad _____

ropes _____

races _____

mares _____

stable _____

asleep _____

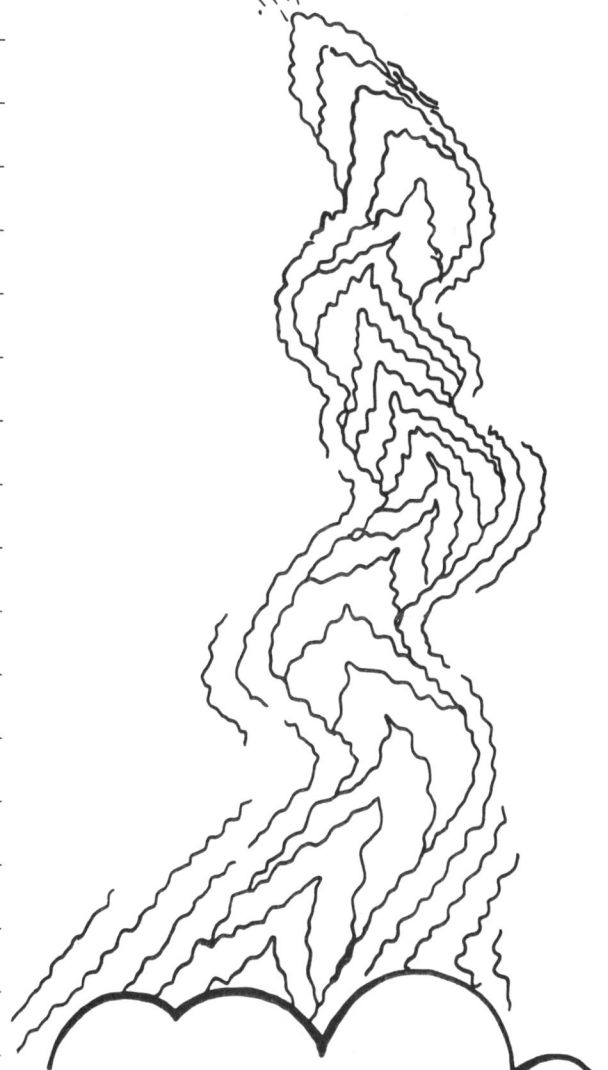

Name: _____

Find anagrams for these words and see if you can fly your rocket back to Earth.

1   Look at the letters in each word.
2   Rearrange all of the letters to form a new word. This is an 'anagram'.
3   Write the anagram in the space provided.
4   For each correct anagram colour in one of the sections in the rocket's trail.
5   If all your answers were correct, you should get back to Earth with fuel to spare.

WoRd STRetchers

ANAGRAMS
ACTIVITY
SHEET 2

sag _____

add _____

dab _____

tip _____

sang _____

mats _____

name _____

yard _____

save _____

race _____

trap _____

cone _____

never _____

state _____

least _____

vales _____

clean _____

table _____

detest _____

rivets _____

Name: _____

Find anagrams for these words and see if you can fly your rocket back to Earth.

1 Look at the letters in each word.
2 Rearrange all of the letters to form a new word. This is an 'anagram'.
3 Write the anagram in the space provided.
4 For each correct anagram colour in one of the sections in the rocket's trail.
5 If all your answers were correct, you should get back to Earth with fuel to spare.

net _____

but _____

pea _____

owe _____

cane _____

plug _____

grin _____

rate _____

sole _____

tide _____

halt _____

draw _____

parts _____

cheat _____

glare _____

groan _____

notes _____

waste _____

master _____

battle _____

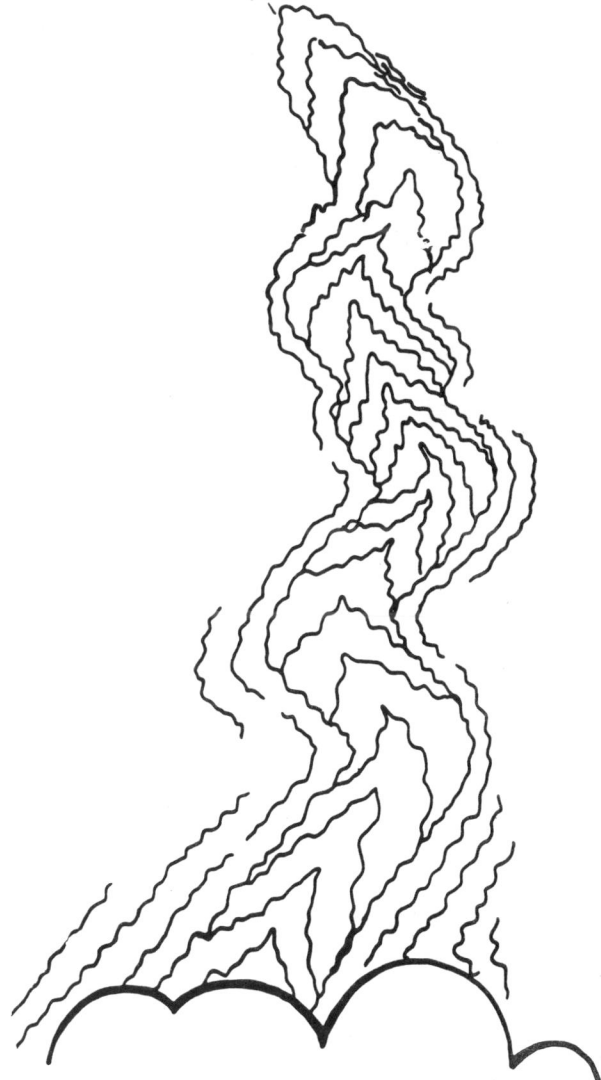

Name: _____

Find anagrams for these words and see if you can fly your rocket back to Earth.

1 Look at the letters in each word.
2 Rearrange all of the letters to form a new word. This is an 'anagram'.
3 Write the anagram in the space provided.
4 For each correct anagram colour in one of the sections in the rocket's trail.
5 If all your answers were correct, you should get back to Earth with fuel to spare.

WoRd STRetchers

ANAGRAMS
ACTIVITY
SHEET 4

car _____

owl _____

dew _____

who _____

rots _____

west _____

part _____

bale _____

hose _____

goat _____

lies _____

laze _____

rats _____

cents _____

spate _____

great _____

plate _____

foster _____

pierce _____

stinger _____

Name: _____

These 10 'sound' words form a set of steps. Can you make similar sets of steps for animals and household items?

1 Arrange your words in steps, with the last letter of one word being the first letter of the next. (Use the back of the sheet if you need more space.)

2 All words must relate to the topic.

3 Words must be spelt correctly. Use your dictionary if in doubt.

4 Can you make a run of 10 words?

5 Score one point for each word (Total: 20)

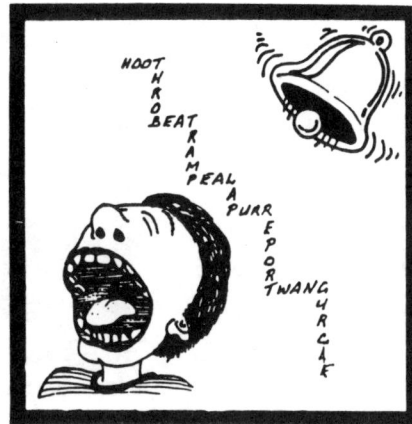

Topic: Sound

Topic: Animals, for example, gazelle, elk

Topic: Household items, for example, carpet, television

Colour the activity page and then write in the number of points you scored.

Name: _____

These 10 'sound' words form a set of steps. Can you make similar sets of steps for clothes and food?

1   Arrange your words in steps, with the last letter of one word being the first letter of the next. (Use the back of the sheet if you need more space.)

2   All words must relate to the topic.

3   Words must be spelt correctly. Use your dictionary if in doubt.

4   Can you make a run of 10 words?

5   Score one point for each word (Total: 20)

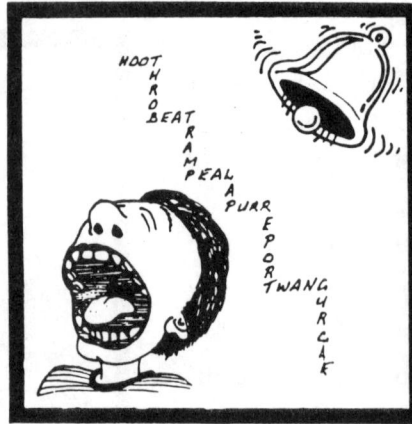

Topic: Sound

Topic: Clothes, for example, scar**f**, **f**rock

Topic: Food, for example, avocad**o**, **o**nion

Colour the activity page and then write in the number of points you scored.

Name: _____

These 10 'sound' words form a set of steps. Can you make similar sets of steps for body parts and occupations?

1 Arrange your words in steps, with the last letter of one word being the first letter of the next. (Use the back of the sheet if you need more space.)

2 All words must relate to the topic.

3 Words must be spelt correctly. Use your dictionary if in doubt.

4 Can you make a run of 10 words?

5 Score one point for each word (Total: 20)

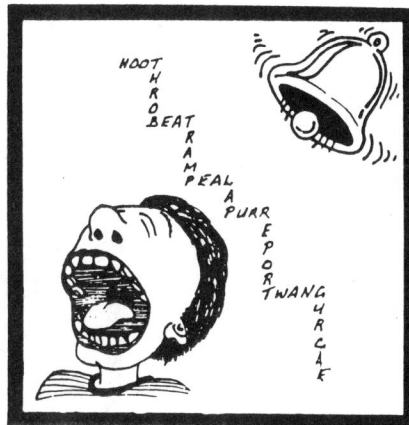

Topic: Sound

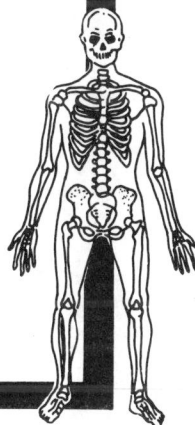

Topic: Body parts, for example, femur, rib

Topic: Occupations, for example, nurse, engineer

Colour the activity page and the write in the number of points you scored.

WoRd STRetchers

STEP IT OUT

ACTIVITY SHEET 3

Name: _____

These 10 'sound' words form a set of steps. Can you make similar sets of steps for sports and tools?

1 Arrange your words in steps, with the last letter of one word being the first letter of the next. (Use the back of the sheet if you need more space.)

2 All words must relate to the topic.

3 Words must be spelt correctly. Use your dictionary if in doubt.

4 Can you make a run of 10 words?

5 Score one point for each word (Total: 20)

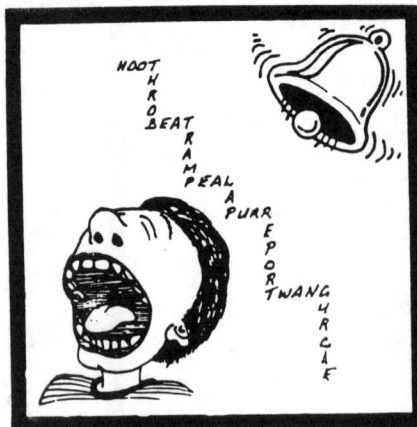

Topic: Sound

Topic: Sports, for example, tennis, squash

Topic: Tools, for example, saw, wrench

Colour the activity page and then write in the number of points you scored.

Name: _____

These ten words are connected by 'Link Letters' for the topic water sports. Can you make a similar word chain for sports and colour?

1 Arrange your words on the grid so that they are correctly linked together. Any letter other than the first letter of the previous word may be used to begin a word.

2 All words must relate to the topic.

3 Words must be spelt correctly. Use your dictionary if in doubt.

4 Can you make a word chain containing 10 words that fits within the grid?

5 Score one point for each word (Total: 20).

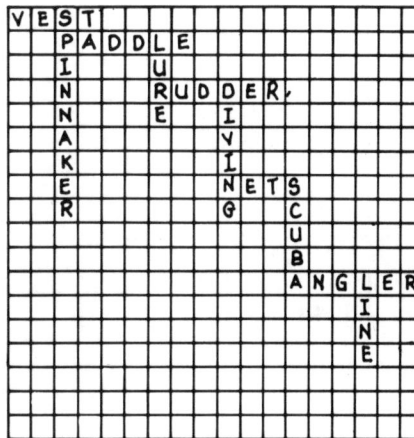

Topic: Water sports

WoRd STRetchers

LINK
LETTERS
ACTIVITY SHEET 1

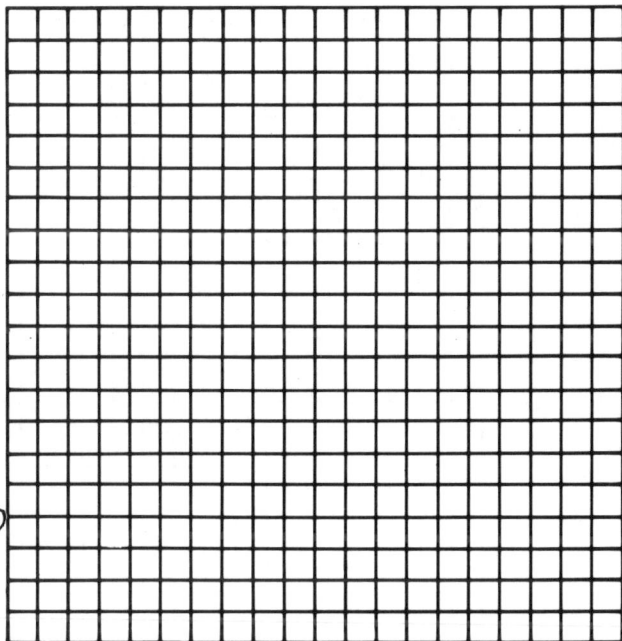

Topic: Sports, for example, golf, football

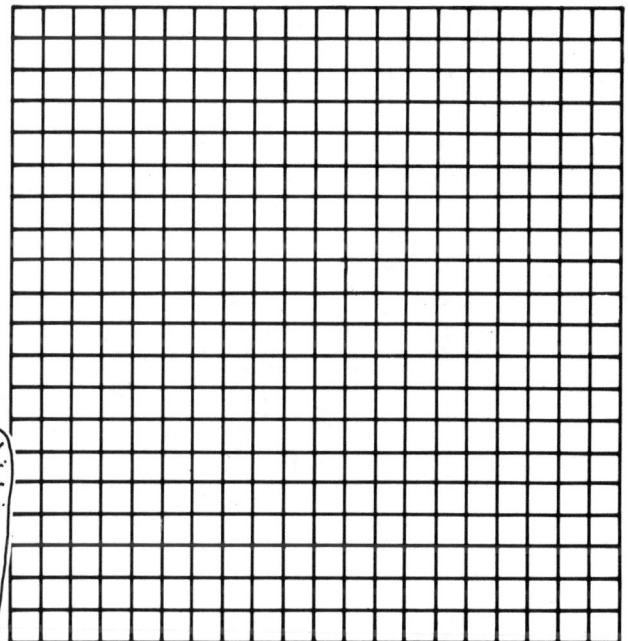

Topic: Colour words, for example, brown, orange

Colour the activity page and then colour in this snake. Colour one segment for each point scored. Did you colour the whole snake?

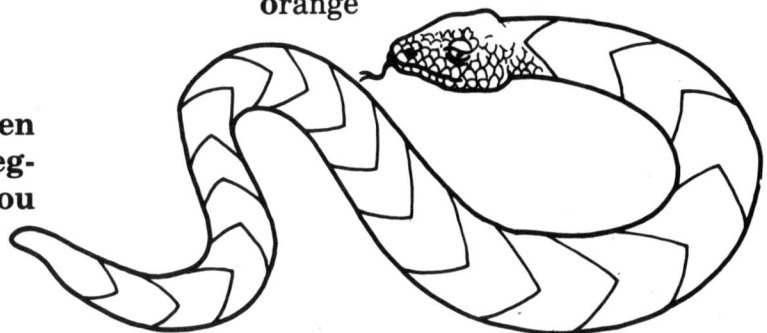

Name: _____

These ten words are connected by 'Link Letters' for the topic water sports. Can you make a similar word chain for farming and school?

1. Arrange your words on the grid so that they are correctly linked together. Any letter other than the first letter of the previous word may be used to begin a word.

2. All words must relate to the topic.

3. Words must be spelt correctly. Use your dictionary if in doubt.

4. Can you make a word chain containing 10 words that fits within the grid?

5. Score one point for each word (Total: 20).

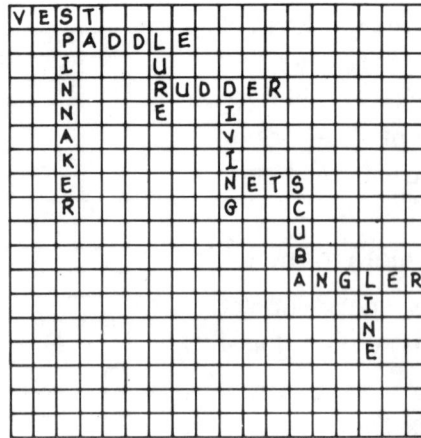

Topic: Water sports

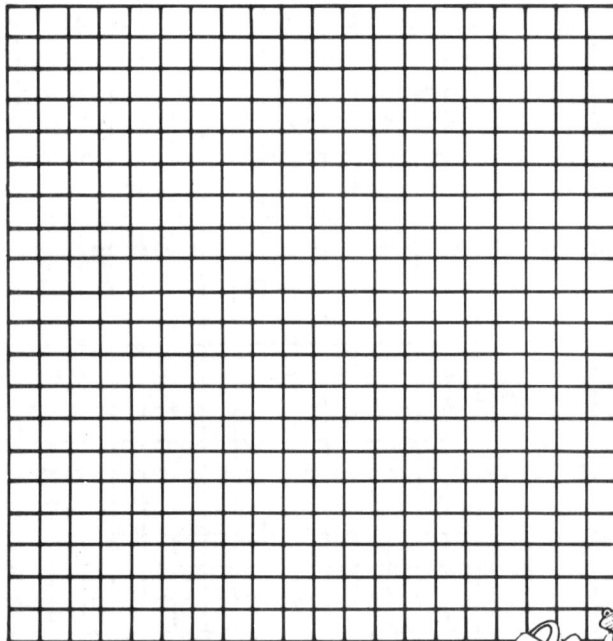

Topic: Farming, for example, sheep, herd

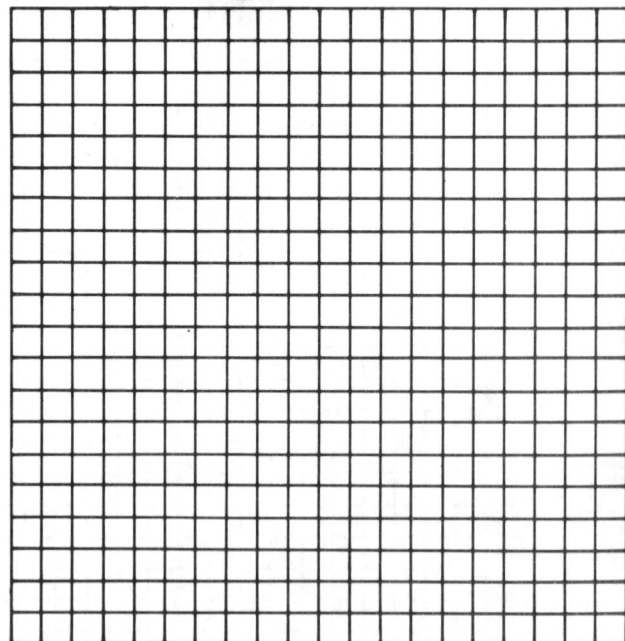

Topic: School, for example, teacher, homework

Colour the activity page and then colour in this snake. Colour one segment for each point scored. Did you colour the whole snake?

Name: _____

These ten words are connected by 'Link Letters', for the topic water sports. Can you make a similar word chain for feelings and eating?

1 Arrange your words on the grid so that they are correctly linked together. Any letter other than the first letter of the previous word may be used to begin a word.

2 All words must relate to the topic.

3 Words must be spelt correctly. Use your dictionary if in doubt.

4 Can you make a word chain containing 10 words that fits within the grid?

5 Score one point for each word (Total: 20).

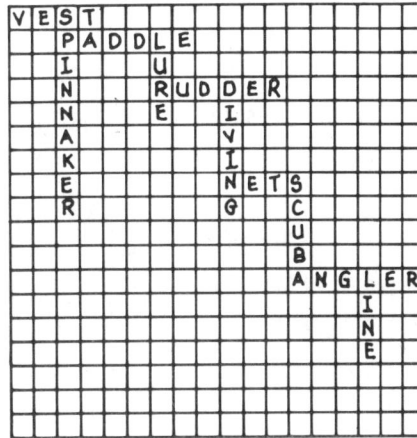

Topic: Water sports

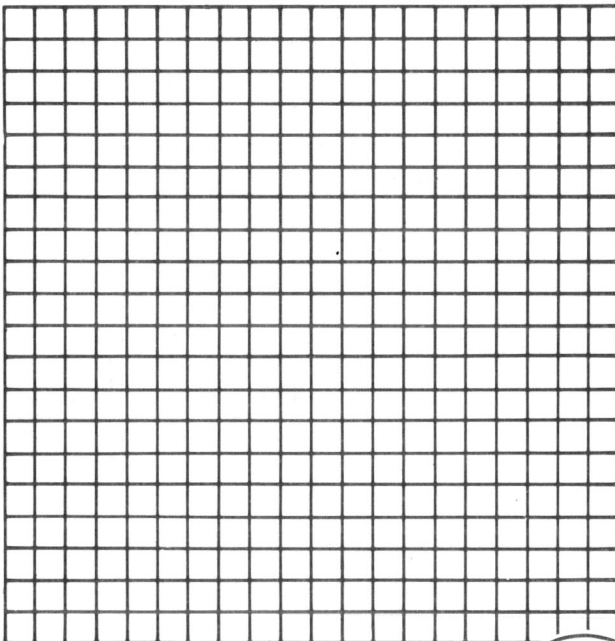

Topic: Feelings, for example, pleased, sad

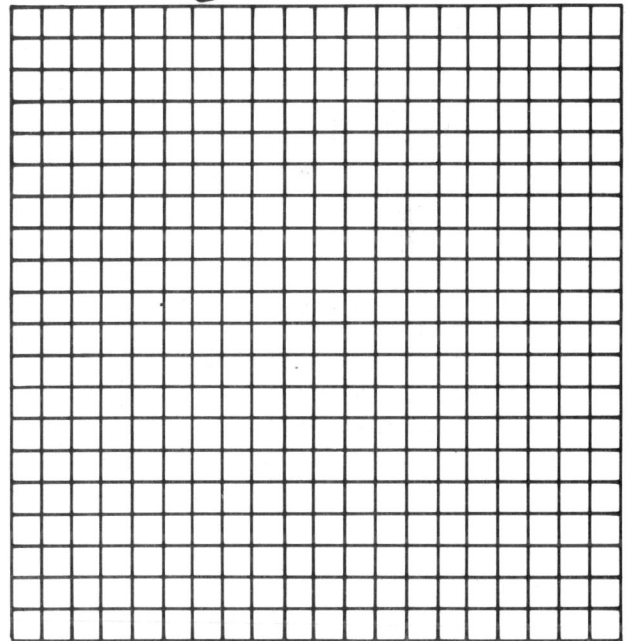

Topic: Eating, for example, dinner, napkin

Colour the activity page and then colour in this snake. Colour one segment for each point scored. Did you colour the whole snake?

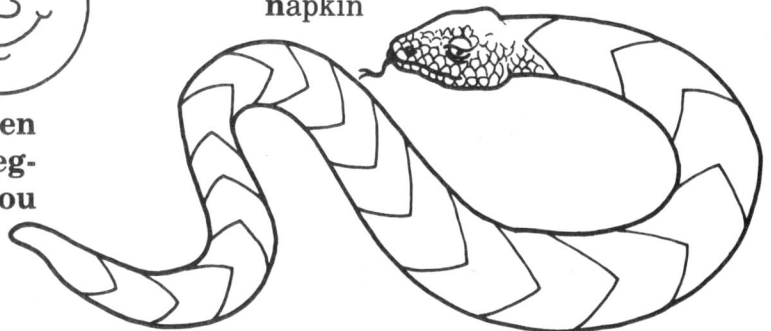

23

Name: _____

These ten words are connected by 'Link Letters' for the topic water sports. Can you make a similar word chain for careers and show time?

1 Arrange your words on the grid so that they are correctly linked together. Any letter other than the first letter of the previous word may be used to begin a word.

2 All words must relate to the topic.

3 Words must be spelt correctly. Use your dictionary if in doubt.

4 Can you make a word chain containing 10 words that fits within the grid?

5 Score one point for each word (Total: 20).

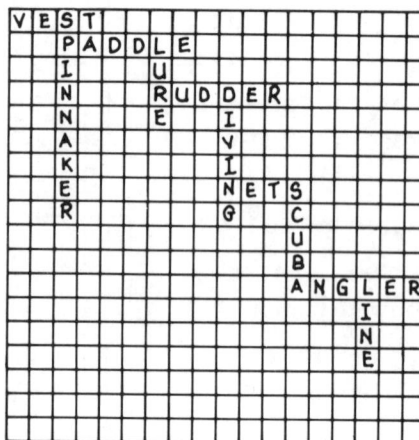

Topic: Water sports

V	E	S	T										
	P	A	D	D	L	E							
	I		U										
	N		R	U	D	D	E	R					
	N		E		I								
	A				V								
	K				I								
	E				N	E	T	S					
	R				G			C					
								U					
								B					
							A	N	G	L	E	R	
									I				
									N				
									E				

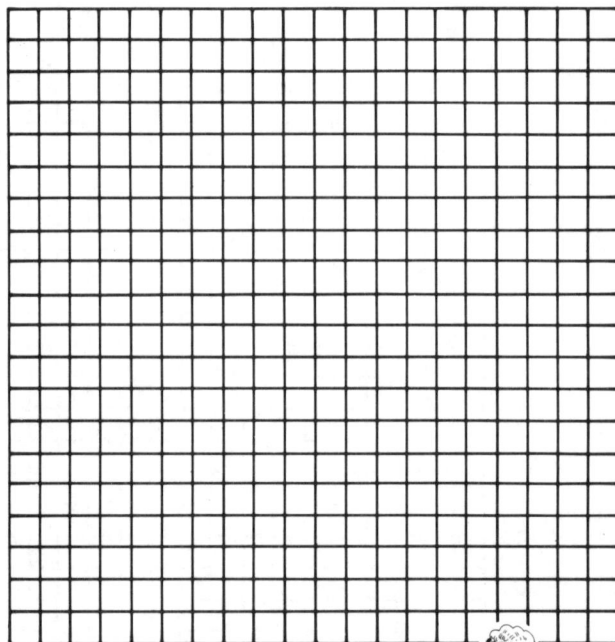

Topic: Careers, for example, teacher, carpenter

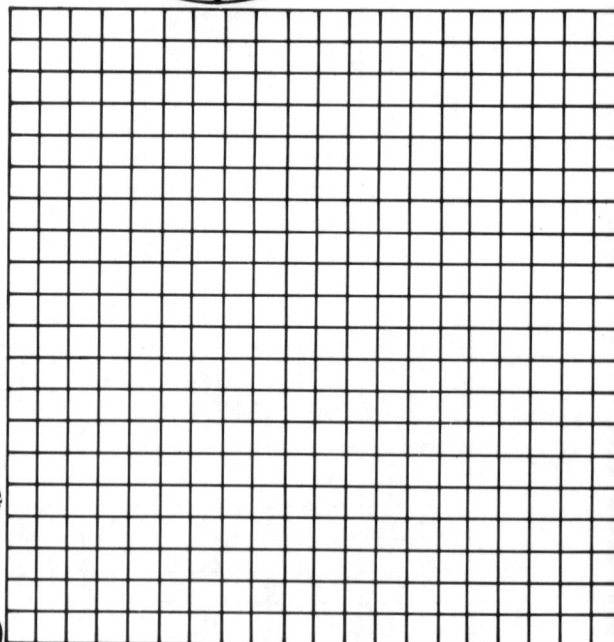

Topic: Show time words, for example, orchestra, curtain

Colour the activity page and then colour in this snake. Colour one segment for each point scored. Did you colour the whole snake?

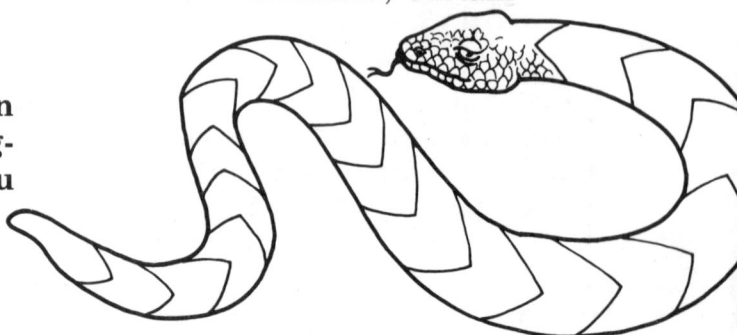

Name: _____

Can you beat the barrier? How long does it take you to unjumble these words?

1 Each of these letter-groups can be rejuggled to form a real word.

2 Write your word beside the set of letters.

3 Note: There may be more than one acceptable answer.

4 If in doubt about a word, use your dictionary.

5 Play until 'time' is called.

Colour the activity sheet. If you finished before the time was up, record how long you took on the clock below.

If you have time, make up your own set of jumbled words and give them to a classmate.

WoRd STRetchers

BEAT THE BARRIER

ACTIVITY SHEET 1

TEL _____

APM _____

RIHA _____

IMKL _____

GREIT _____

HTIFA _____

MYNEE _____

EINRPC _____

TRAEMK _____

NTTIAOS _____

Name: _____

Can you beat the barrier? How long does it take you to unjumble these words?

1 Each of these letter-groups can be rejuggled to form a real word.

2 Write your word beside the set of letters.

3 Note: There may be more than one acceptable answer.

4 If in doubt about a word, use your dictionary.

5 Play until 'time' is called.

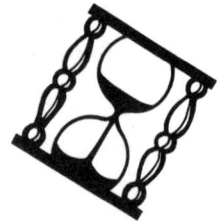

Colour the activity sheet. If you finished before the time was up, record how long you took on the clock below.

If you have time, make up your own set of jumbled words and give them to a classmate.

BOF	_____
GRU	_____
POEH	_____
RDAO	_____
PPYAL	_____
XLARE	_____
TIOLP	_____
ICOFEF	_____
SOPREN	_____
RRAELGU	_____

WoRd STRetchers

BEAT THE BARRIER

ACTIVITY SHEET 2

Name: _____

Can you beat the barrier? How long does it take you to unjumble these words?

1 Each of these letter-groups can be rejuggled to form a real word.

2 Write your word beside the set of letters.

3 Note: There may be more than one acceptable answer.

4 If in doubt about a word, use your dictionary.

5 Play until 'time' is called.

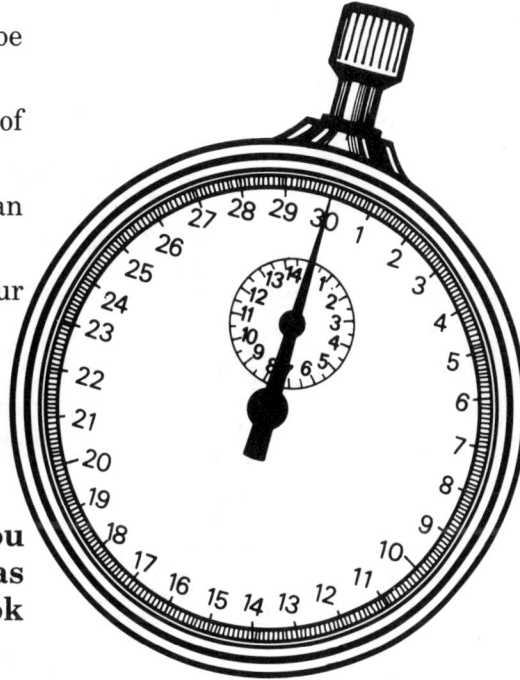

Colour the activity sheet. If you finished before the time was up, record how long you took on the clock below.

If you have time, make up your own set of jumbled words and give them to a classmate.

AWP	_____
AEG	_____
SNWE	_____
YJRU	_____
LEEVA	_____
TBIOR	_____
LLGAE	_____
STEECR	_____
HETNGL	_____
TTDSNUE	_____

Name: _____

Can you beat the barrier? How long does it take you to unjumble these words?

1 Each of these letter-groups can be rejuggled to form a real word.

2 Write your word beside the set of letters.

3 Note: There may be more than one acceptable answer.

4 If in doubt about a word, use your dictionary.

5 Play until 'time' is called.

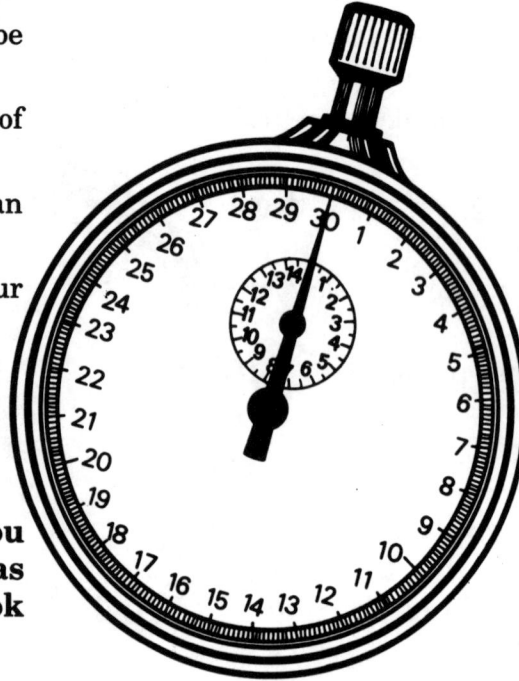

Colour the activity sheet. If you finished before the time was up, record how long you took on the clock below.

If you have time, make up your own set of jumbled words and give them to a classmate.

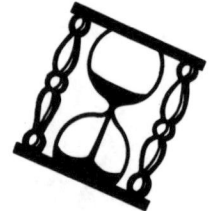

BOS _____

DAW _____

REOC _____

DAEI _____

HREOC _____

OOTTM _____

DTIEB _____

CHREAS _____

WRDREA _____

TACEINN _____

Name: _____

All 25 words listed below are lost in this jumble of letters. How many can you find?

1 The words are written either left to right or downwards.

2 Letters may be shared between words. Draw a line through each word that you find in the grid.

3 Each time you find a word, colour in the first box.

4 If you know the meaning of the word (or have checked it in the dictionary), colour in the second box.

5 How well did you go?

```
Z F P D B E M S U Y Z J X A
H Q G R A N D M O T H E R B
U S A A D O L E S C E N T R
S Z X O P R X G L W C I O T
B D Q F B O O V I Q H E B R
A F F M A N R O N J I C T H
N A E O S I S T E R L E E E
D T M M B A B Y P C D X E R
W H A O D A U G H T E R N J
I E L T L M A L E I V A U N
D R E H A S O N W K P A G C
O P Y E D I N F A N T U E L
W M O R Y S P O U S E L R E
W I F E Z Y A U N T R T N E
```

Faces			
0–5	6–10	11–15	16–20

21–25

Colour the activity page, highlighting the face that shows how well you did with this activity.

Adolescent		
Adult		
Aunt		
Baby		
Brother		
Child		
Daughter		
Father		
Female		
Grandmother		
Husband		
Infant		
Lady		
Male		
Man		
Mother		
Nephew		
Niece		
Sister		
Son		
Spouse		
Teenager		
Uncle		
Widow		
Wife		

Name: _____

All 24 words listed below are lost in this jumble of letters. How many can you find?

1. The words are written either left to right, downwards or diagonally (to the right).

2. Letters may be shared between words. Draw a line through each word that you find in the grid.

3. Each time you find a word, colour in the first box.

4. If you know the meaning of the word (or have checked it in the dictionary), colour in the second box.

5. How well did you go?

WORD STRETCHERS

MISSING WORDS!
ACTIVITY SHEET 2

```
G I R P S L C L F U V X A C
F W K P A Z A B O B X Y T A
Q E I L G S Y U E U D R T R
E N T R Y R S L N D N O I P
C J G V E B E A O D R G C O
S O A N E T A E G B R O E R
P M R R T R D T N E B Y O T
A E A R E O A R H H Q Y M M
F B G D I N I N G R O O M J
L K E S O D W L D P O U B X
C E L L A R O D E A O O S S
K I T C H E N R E T H R M E
P L V E S T I B U L E X C A
H A L L S H O W E R Y U R H
```

Attic		
Bar		
Bathroom		
Bedroom		
Carport		
Cellar		
Corridor		
Diningroom		
Entry		
Fernery		
Garage		
Greenhouse		
Hall		
Kitchen		
Laundry		
Lobby		
Lounge		
Passage		
Porch		
Shower		
Spa		
Toilet		
Verandah		
Vestibule		

0–5   6–10   11–15   16–20

21–24

Colour the activity page, highlighting the face that shows how well you did with this activity.

Name: _____

All 25 words listed below are lost in this jumble of letters. How many can you find?

1 The words are written forwards, backwards, upwards, downwards or diagonally.

2 Letters may be shared between words. Draw a line through each word that you find in the grid.

3 Each time you find a word, colour in the first box.

4 If you know the meaning of the word (or have checked it in the dictionary), colour in the second box.

5 How well did you go?

WoRd STRetchers

MISSING WORDS!
ACTIVITY SHEET 3

H	C	W	Q	Q	T	R	A	I	N	S	W	S	E
E	U	C	I	E	F	H	Q	G	W	T	H	C	U
N	R	R	E	N	C	G	N	P	T	O	A	Y	T
O	D	L	R	L	D	I	J	S	W	R	X	E	D
L	S	R	R	I	N	W	A	E	Y	M	M	W	R
C	F	Y	A	T	C	C	R	T	B	P	E	O	I
Y	K	G	H	Z	R	A	I	W	E	D	T	B	Z
C	O	G	E	E	Z	D	N	R	R	H	O	N	Z
F	I	E	V	F	I	I	A	E	U	V	D	I	L
L	S	O	L	M	W	T	L	N	L	F	A	A	E
D	I	O	U	A	U	O	D	B	R	C	N	R	T
F	O	H	C	R	G	E	N	O	H	O	R	R	S
D	N	I	E	A	R	Y	S	S	C	U	O	S	I
Q	C	L	O	U	D	T	L	I	A	H	T	L	M

Blizzard
Cloud
Cyclone
Dew
Drizzle
Flood
Fog
Frost
Gale
Hail
Humidity
Hurricane
Lightning
Mist
Overcast
Rain
Rainbow
Shower
Sleet
Snow
Storm
Temperature
Thunder
Tornado
Wind

0–5   6–10   11–15   16–20

Colour the activity page, highlighting the face that shows how well you did with this activity.

21–25

31

Name: _____

All 24 words listed below are lost in this jumble of letters. How many can you find?

1 The words are written forwards, backwards, upwards, downwards or diagonally.

2 Letters may be shared between words. Draw a line through each word that you find in the grid.

3 Each time you find a word, colour in the first box.

4 If you know the meaning of the word (or have checked it in the dictionary), colour in the second box.

5 How well did you go?

```
C C K O X Y G E N S F U E C
O Y G I I U L R S P T T L R
N T D X N U K A Y A O E U A
T I X E D T T K M C R K S F
R V I O S E U A I E B C P T
O A M T L I L P H S I O A S
L R G L U T R P S H T R P S
X G I N I A S U M I I H S A
A T H T I O N I S P A H V C
E P U C M D S O E S U L R E
C D O T N S N B R T E A F S
E D A L I U O A T T N R H U
N A F O L R A L L U S X P I
B P N O P O E L L J D A D T
```

0–5   6–10   11–15   16–20

Colour the activity page, highlighting the face that shows how well you did with this activity.

21–24

Altitude
Apollo
Astronaut
Atmosphere
Capsule
Control
Craft
Gravity
Landing
Launch
Lunar
Mission
Module
Orbit
Oxygen
Pad
Pressurised
Probe
Rocket
Satellite
Shuttle
Spaceship
Spacesuit
Sputnik

Name: _____

How many of these alphabetic anagrams can you solve? How high can you hit the clanger?

1 Look at the base word.

2 Add the given letter of the alphabet to this word.

3 Rearrange all of the letters to form a new word.

4 Write the new word in the space provided.

5 Total the number of anagralphabets that you were able to make.

6 This shows how high you can hit the Clanger.

Colour the activity page and show how high you hit your clanger.

WoRd STRetchers

ANA-GRALPHABETS

ACTIVITY SHEET 1

Clang!

A +test	=_____
B +ran	=_____
C +ten	=_____
D +ear	=_____
E +had	=_____
F +ram	=_____
G +lean	=_____
H +nut	=_____
I +nor	=_____
J +yell	=_____
K +sir	=_____
L +map	=_____
M+sit	=_____
N +drab	=_____
O +nest	=_____
P +mud	=_____
Q +suit	=_____
R +tie	=_____
S +had	=_____
T +seen	=_____
U +its	=_____
V +die	=_____
W+has	=_____
X +eon	=_____
Y +ram	=_____
Z +ore	=_____

WOW!
26

25 24 23 22 21 20 19 18 17 16 15 14 13 12 11 10 9 8 7 6 5 4 3 2 1 0

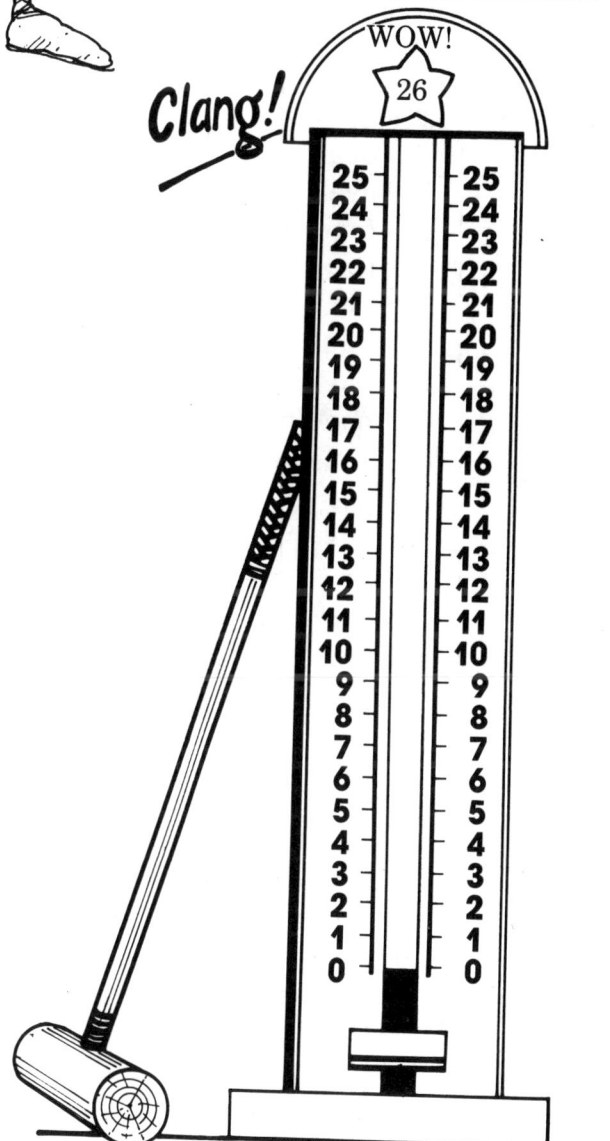

33

Name: _____

How many of these alphabetic anagrams can you solve? How high can you hit the clanger?

1 Look at the base word.

2 Add the given letter of the alphabet to this word.

3 Rearrange all of the letters to form a new word.

4 Write the new word in the space provided.

5 Total the number of anagralphabets that you were able to make.

6 This shows how high you can hit the Clanger.

Colour the activity page and show how high you hit your clanger.

WoRd STRetchers

ANA-GRALPHABETS

ACTIVITY SHEET 2

Clang!

WOW!
26

A +stew =	_____
B +dear =	_____
C +over =	_____
D +tea =	_____
E +farm =	_____
F +stir =	_____
G +haul =	_____
H +die =	_____
I +noon =	_____
J +stole =	_____
K +pet =	_____
L +day =	_____
M+lies =	_____
N +sure =	_____
O +port =	_____
P +toil =	_____
Q +suet =	_____
R +mud =	_____
S +tea =	_____
T +coin =	_____
U +tin =	_____
V +sat =	_____
W+ram =	_____
X +real =	_____
Y +lets =	_____
Z +bare =	_____

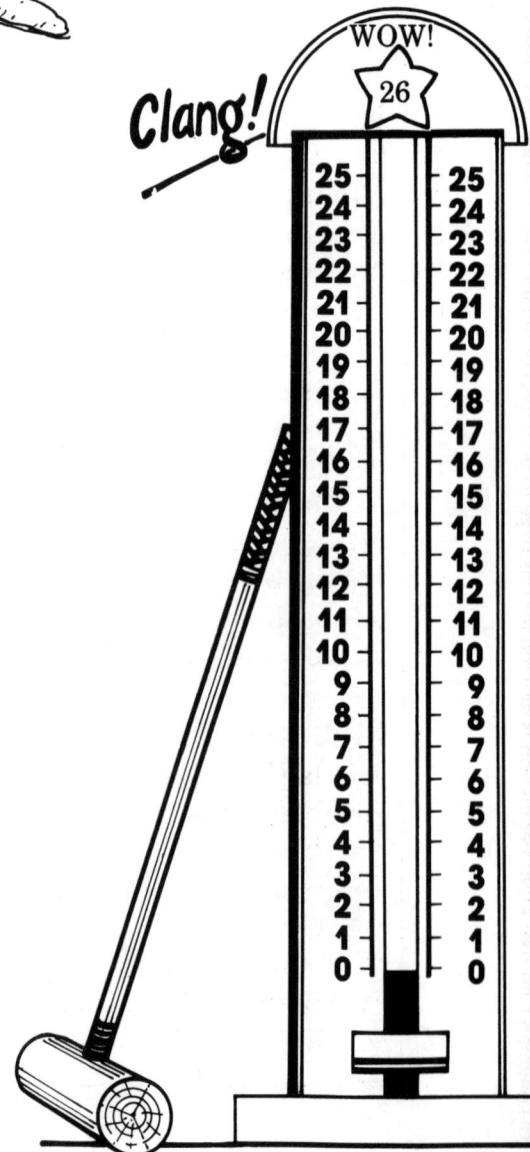

Name: _____

How many of these alphabetic anagrams can you solve? How high can you hit the clanger?

1 Look at the base word.

2 Add the given letter of the alphabet to this word.

3 Rearrange all of the letters to form a new word.

4 Write the new word in the space provided.

5 Total the number of anagralphabets that you were able to make.

6 This shows how high you can hit the Clanger.

Colour the activity page and show how high you hit your clanger.

A +rope = _____
B +read = _____
C +real = _____
D +heat = _____
E +mast = _____
F +cart = _____
G +spar = _____
H +pace = _____
I +nose = _____
J +into = _____
K +tin   = _____
L +beat = _____
M+deal   = _____
N +love = _____
O +rang = _____
P +snore = _____
Q +suit = _____
R +made = _____
S +lags = _____
T +bed   = _____
U +boat = _____
V +teen = _____
W+tear   = _____
X +tear = _____
Y +roam = _____
Z +ale   = _____

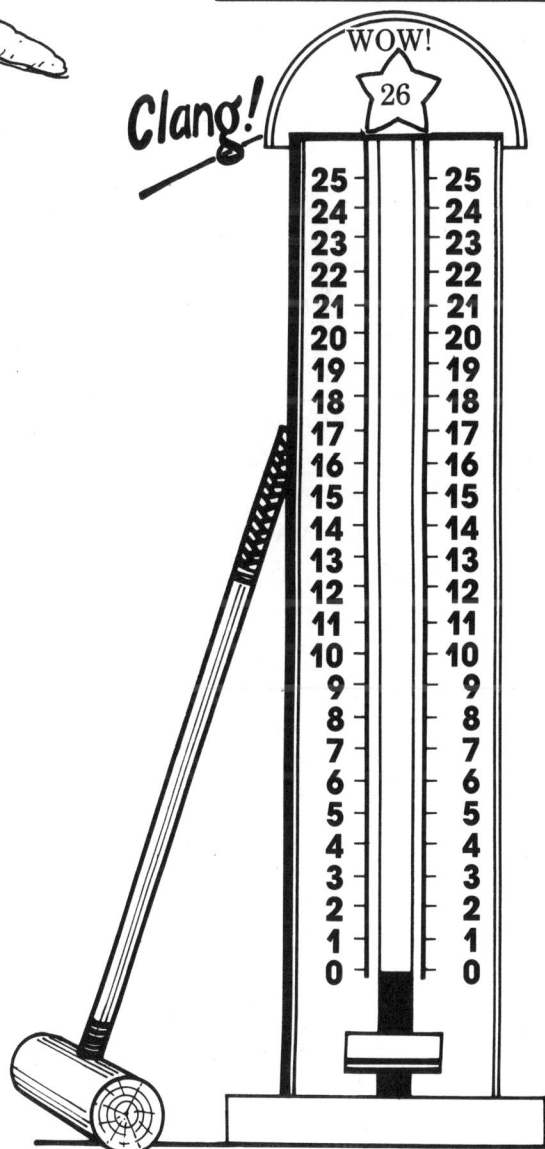

Clang!

WOW!
26

25 25
24 24
23 23
22 22
21 21
20 20
19 19
18 18
17 17
16 16
15 15
14 14
13 13
12 12
11 11
10 10
9 9
8 8
7 7
6 6
5 5
4 4
3 3
2 2
1 1
0 0

Name: _____

How many of these alphabetic anagrams can you solve? How high can you hit the clanger?

1　Look at the base word.

2　Add the given letter of the alphabet to this word.

3　Rearrange all of the letters to form a new word.

4　Write the new word in the space provided.

5　Total the number of anagralphabets that you were able to make.

6　This shows how high you can hit the Clanger.

Colour the activity page and show how high you hit your clanger.

WoRd STRetchers

ANA-GRALPHABETS

ACTIVITY SHEET 4

A +beat = _____
B +late = _____
C +hate = _____
D +trees = _____
E +seat = _____
F +store = _____
G +coil = _____
H +tore = _____
I +pulp = _____
J +glean = _____
K +peas = _____
L +rage = _____
M +stare = _____
N +veer = _____
O +hat = _____
P +liars = _____
Q +suet = _____
R +stare = _____
S +mare = _____
T +great = _____
U +red = _____
V +liar = _____
W +seat = _____
X +dime = _____
Y +chat = _____
Z +oboe = _____

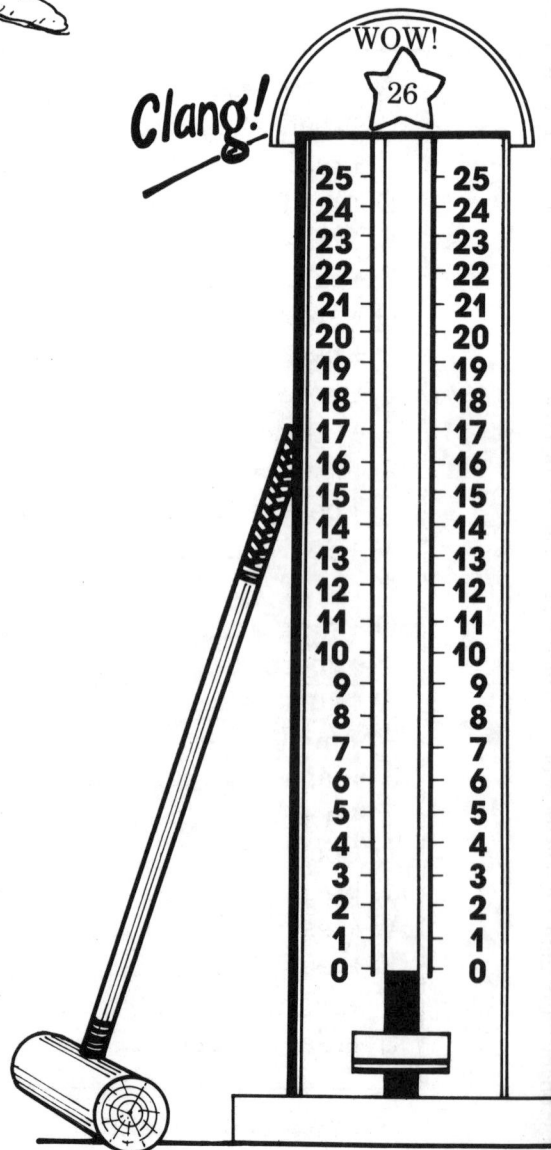

Clang!

WOW!
26

25 · 25
24 · 24
23 · 23
22 · 22
21 · 21
20 · 20
19 · 19
18 · 18
17 · 17
16 · 16
15 · 15
14 · 14
13 · 13
12 · 12
11 · 11
10 · 10
9 · 9
8 · 8
7 · 7
6 · 6
5 · 5
4 · 4
3 · 3
2 · 2
1 · 1
0 · 0

Name: _____

Can you pull 20 words out of this hat?

1 List your words in the spaces provided.

2 The words must relate to the theme.

3 Where letters are provided they must be built into the word, that is, think of an occupation that begins with the letters set out below.

Colour in the activity page and tick which response you think your mum would make if she saw your work.

If my mum saw my work she'd say it was:

- unbelievable
- totally believable
- revolting
- obviously not mine
- too good to be true
- grotesque

a _____	l _____
b _____	m _____
c _____	n _____
d _____	o _____
e _____	p _____
f _____	r _____
g _____	s _____
h _____	u _____
i _____	v _____
j _____	z _____

Theme: Occupations

Name: _____

Can you pull 20 words out of this hat?

1 List your words in the spaces provided.

2 The words must relate to the theme.

3 Where letters are provided they must be built into the word, that is, think of animals that end with the letters set out below.

Colour in the activity page and tick which response you think your mum would make if she saw your work.

If my mum saw my work she'd say it was:

- unbelievable
- totally believable
- revolting
- obviously not mine
- too good to be true
- grotesque

WoRd STRetchers

TWENTY WORDS

ACTIVITY SHEET 2

a _____

b _____

d _____

e _____

f _____

g _____

h _____

k _____

l _____

m _____

n _____

o _____

p _____

r _____

s _____

t _____

u _____

w _____

x _____

y _____

Theme: Animals

Name: _____

WoRd
STRetchers

TWENTY
WORDS

ACTIVITY
SHEET 3

Can you pull 20 words out of this hat?

1   List your words in the spaces provided.

2   The words must relate to the theme.

3   Where letters are provided they must be built into the word, that is, think of fruit and vegetables that begin or end with the letters set out below.

Colour in the activity page and tick which response you think your mum would make if she saw your work.

If my mum saw my work she'd say it was:

- unbelievable
- totally believable
- revolting
- obviously not mine
- too good to be true
- grotesque

a _____ o

b _____

c

d _____

e

f _____

g _____

h

i

l _____

m _____

n

o

p _____

q _____

r

s

t

w

y

Theme: Fruit and Vegetables

Name: _____

Can you pull 20 words out of this hat?

1 List your words in the spaces provided.

2 The words must relate to the theme.

3 Where letters are provided they must be built into the word, that is, at the beginning, in the middle or at the end of the word.

Colour in the activity page and tick which response you think your mum would make if she saw your work.

If my mum saw my work she'd say it was:

- unbelievable
- totally believable
- revolting
- obviously not mine
- too good to be true
- grotesque

WoRd STRetchers

TWENTY WORDS ACTIVITY SHEET 4

a _____

b _____

cc _____

g-g _____

ii _____

k _____

ll _____

mn _____

nn _____

oo _____

q _____

f r _____

h _____

v _____

w _____

x _____

Theme: Sports

Name: _____

Can you complete this cross grid?

1 Fill in the grid with words of your own choice, scoring points for each letter used (see the table for the point value of each letter). Letters falling on a cross score points in both words.

2 As you are trying to gain as many points as possible, keep looking for better-scoring words.

3 If you are not sure of a word's spelling, check it in a dictionary.

4 Look at the example cross grid before you begin.

Example: cross grid

Colour in the activity page and highlight on the scoreboard the number of points you scored.

$A_1 \ B_4 \ C_4 \ D_2 \ E_1 \ F_4 \ G_3 \ H_4 \ I_1$
$J_5 \ K_2 \ L_2 \ M_3 \ N_2 \ O_1 \ P_3 \ Q_8 \ R_2$
$S_2 \ T_2 \ U_1 \ V_5 \ W_4 \ X_6 \ Y_3 \ Z_6$

Scoreboard

Name: _____

Can you complete this cross grid?

1 Fill in the grid with words of your own choice, scoring points for each letter used (see the table for the point value of each letter). Letters falling on a cross score points in both words.

2 As you are trying to gain as many points as possible, keep looking for better-scoring words.

3 If you are not sure of a word's spelling, check it in a dictionary.

4 Look at the example cross grid before you begin.

Example: cross grid

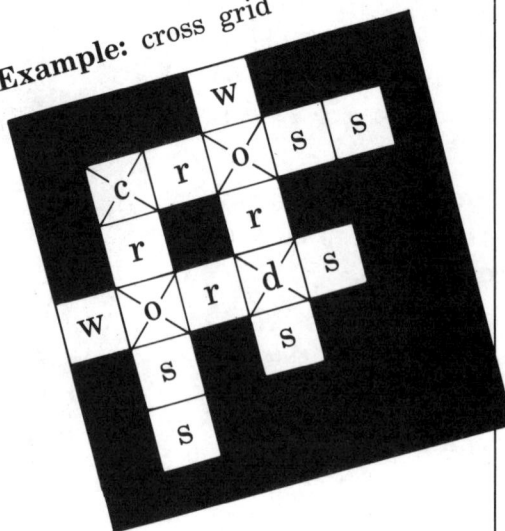

Colour in the activity page and highlight on the score-board the number of points you scored.

$A_1 B_4 C_4 D_2 E_1 F_4 G_3 H_4 I_1$
$J_5 K_2 L_2 M_3 N_2 O_1 P_3 Q_8 R_2$
$S_2 T_2 U_1 V_5 W_4 X_6 Y_3 Z_6$

Scoreboard

Name: _____

Can you complete this cross grid?

1. Fill in the grid with words of your own choice, scoring points for each letter used (see the table for the point value of each letter). Letters falling on a cross score points in both words.

2. As you are trying to gain as many points as possible, keep looking for better-scoring words.

3. If you are not sure of a word's spelling, check it in a dictionary.

4. Look at the example cross grid before you begin.

Example: cross grid

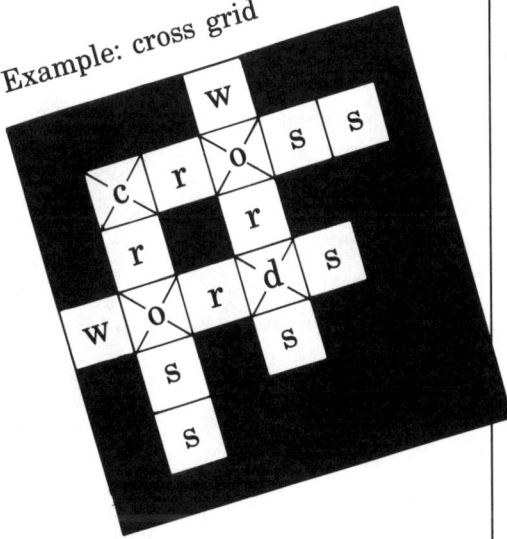

Colour in the activity page and highlight on the scoreboard the number of points you scored.

WoRd STRetchers

CROSS GRIDS ACTIVITY SHEET 3

A_1 B_4 C_4 D_2 E_1 F_4 G_3 H_4 I_1
J_5 K_2 L_2 M_3 N_2 O_1 P_3 Q_8 R_2
S_2 T_2 U_1 V_5 W_4 X_6 Y_3 Z_6

Scoreboard

Name: _____

Can you complete this cross grid?

1 Fill in the grid with words of your own choice, scoring points for each letter used (see the table for the point value of each letter). Letters falling on a cross score points in both words.

2 As you are trying to gain as many points as possible, keep looking for better-scoring words.

3 If you are not sure of a word's spelling, check it in a dictionary.

4 Look at the example cross grid before you begin.

Example: cross grid

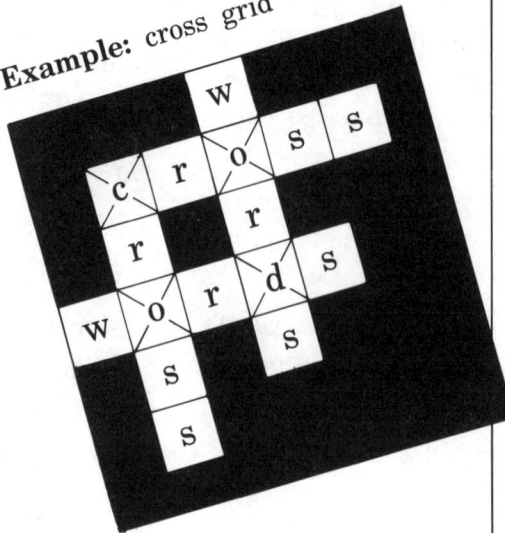

Colour in the activity page and highlight on the scoreboard the number of points you scored.

A_1 B_4 C_4 D_2 E_1 F_4 G_3 H_4 I_1
J_5 K_2 L_2 M_3 N_2 O_1 P_3 Q_8 R_2
S_2 T_2 U_1 V_5 W_4 X_6 Y_3 Z_6

Scoreboard

© Longman Cheshire 1990 Permission is granted for this page to be photocopied for non-commercial classroom use.

Name: _____

Look at this Strip Teaser. How many different words can you make with it?

Imagine the strips of paper can be pulled upwards or downwards, so that each individual letter can be seen through the display frame.

1 Pretend to pull the strips so as to make real words.

2 How many different words can you make? List them on the board.

3 Words must be read from left to right and include all letters shown in the frame.

4 Record your total in the circle.

WoRd STRetchers

STRIP TEASERS

ACTIVITY SHEET 1

B   G
S   N   D
L   E   Y
R   O   T
C   I   N
   A

After colouring the activity page, you might like to try to make up your own Strip Teaser in this frame. How many words can be formed using your Strip Teaser?

Name: _____

Look at this Strip Teaser. How many different words can you make with it?

Imagine the strips of paper can be pulled upwards or downwards, so that each individual letter can be seen through the display frame.

1 Pretend to pull the strips so as to make real words.

2 How many different words can you make? List them on the board.

3 Words must be read from left to right and include all letters shown in the frame.

4 Record your total in the circle.

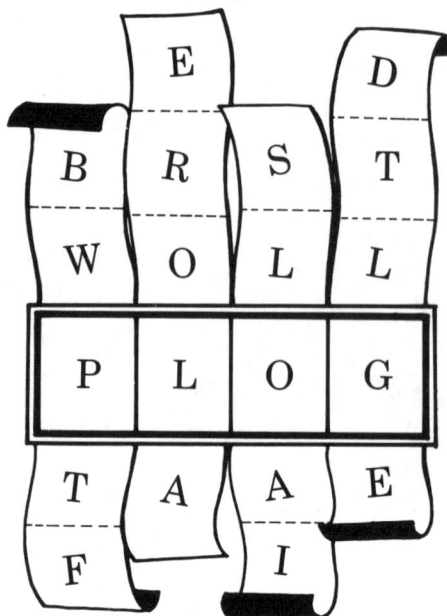

WoRd STREtchers

STRIP TEASERS
ACTIVITY SHEET 2

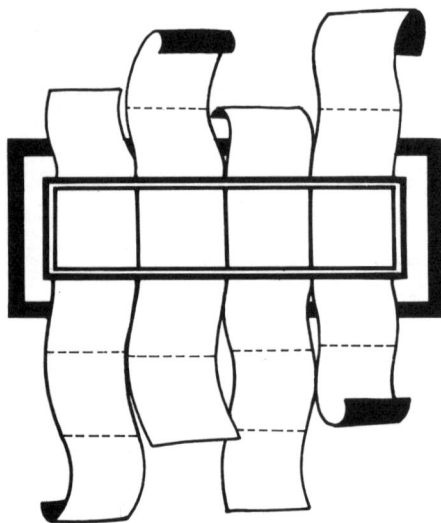

After colouring the activity page, you might like to try to make up your own Strip Teaser in this frame. How many words can be formed using your Strip Teaser?

Name: _____

Look at this Strip Teaser. How many different words can you make with it?

Imagine the strips of paper can be pulled upwards or downwards, so that each individual letter can be seen through the display frame.

1   Pretend to pull the strips so as to make real words.

2   How many different words can you make? List them on the board.

3   Words must be read from left to right and include all letters shown in the frame.

4   Record your total in the circle.

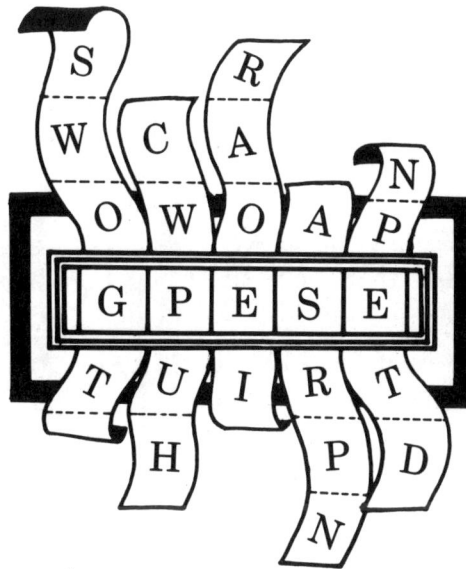

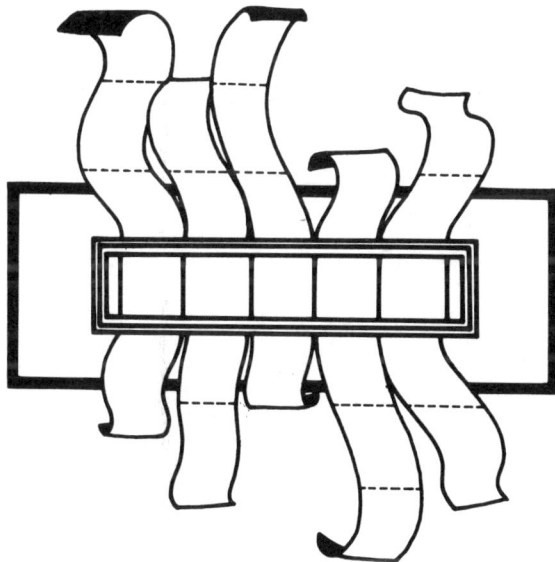

After colouring the activity page, you might like to try to make up your own Strip Teaser in this frame. How many words can be formed using your Strip Teaser?

Name: _____

Look at this Strip Teaser. How many different words can you make with it?

Imagine the strips of paper can be pulled upwards or downwards, so that each individual letter can be seen through the display frame.

1   Pretend to pull the strips so as to make real words.

2   How many different words can you make? List them on the board.

3   Words must be read from left to right and include all letters shown in the frame.

4   Record your total in the circle.

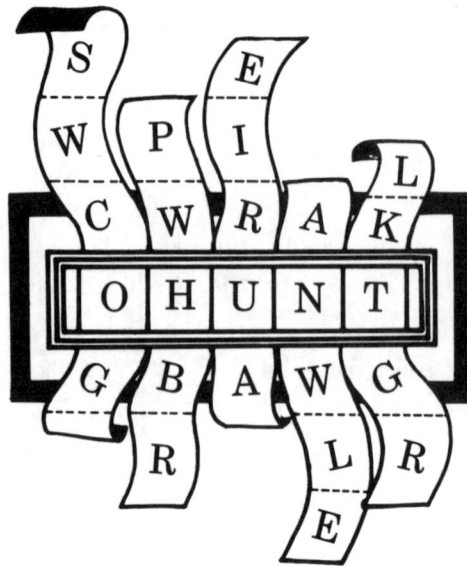

WoRd STRetchers

STRIP TEASERS

ACTIVITY SHEET 4

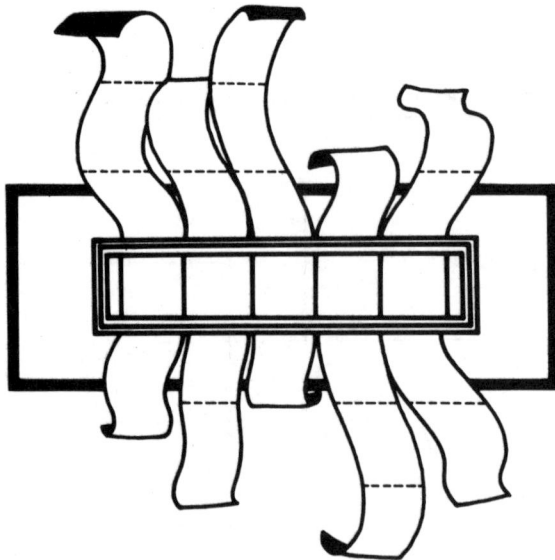

After colouring the activity page, you might like to try to make up your own Strip Teaser in this frame. How many words can be formed using your Strip Teaser?

Name: _____

This is a game of hide-and-seek with a difference. In this game you have to hide as many of the 25 listed words in the grid as you can. How well can you hide them?

1 Write the words in the grid (one letter per square). The words can be written forwards, backwards, upwards, downwards or diagonally.

2 Letters may be shared between words.

3 Fill in the empty squares with letters to hide your words.

4 Each time you hide a word, colour in the first box.

5 If you know the meaning of the word (or have checked it in your dictionary), colour in the second box.

6 How well did you go?

Afternoon
Century
Dawn
Day
Decade
Dusk
Evening
Fortnight
Hour
Midnight
Minute
Month
Morning
Night
Noon
Season
Second
Sunrise
Sunset
Today
Tomorrow
Tonight
Week
Year
Yesterday

0–5   6–10   11–15

16–20   21–25

Colour the activity page, highlighting the award that shows how well you did. Now give your sheet to a classmate to see how many of your words he or she can find.

Name: _____

This is a game of hide-and-seek with a difference. In this game you have to hide as many of the 25 listed words in the grid as you can. How well can you hide them?

1 Write the words in the grid (one letter per square). The words can be written forwards, backwards, upwards, downwards or diagonally.

2 Letters may be shared between words.

3 Fill in the empty squares with letters to hide your words.

4 Each time you hide a word, colour in the first box.

5 If you know the meaning of the word (or have checked it in your dictionary), colour in the second box.

6 How well did you go?

Beret
Blouse
Cap
Cardigan
Coat
Dress
Glove
Hat
Jacket
Jeans
Lingerie
Mitten
Pinafore
Pullover
Pyjamas
Scarf
Shorts
Skirt
Sock
Stockings
Sweater
Tie
Tights
Tunic
Vest

0–5   6–10   11–15

16–20   21–24

Colour the activity page, highlighting the award that shows how well you did. Now give your sheet to a classmate to see how many of your words he or she can find.

50

Name: _____

This is a game of hide-and-seek with a difference. In this game you have to hide as many of the 25 listed words in the grid as you can. How well can you hide them?

1 Write the words in the grid (one letter per square). The words can be written forwards, backwards, upwards, downwards or diagonally.

2 Letters may be shared between words.

3 Fill in the empty squares with letters to hide your words.

4 Each time you hide a word, colour in the first box.

5 If you know the meaning of the word (or have checked it in your dictionary), colour in the second box.

6 How well did you go?

Bay
Channel
Creek
Current
Dam
Delta
Fiord
Gulf
Harbour
Inlet
Lagoon
Lake
Loch
Oasis
Ocean
Reservoir
River
Sea
Spring
Strait
Stream
Tide
Torrent
Tributary
Waves

0–5   6–10   11–15

Colour the activity page, highlighting the award that shows how well you did. Now give your sheet to a classmate to see how many of your words he or she can find.

16–20   21–25

Name: _____

This is a game of hide-and-seek with a difference. In this game you have to hide as many of the 25 listed words in the grid as you can. How well can you hide them?

1 Write the words in the grid (one letter per square). The words can be written forwards, backwards, upwards, downwards or diagonally.

2 Letters may be shared between words.

3 Fill in the empty square with letters to hide your words.

4 Each time you hide a word, colour in the first box.

5 If you know the meaning of the word (or have checked it in your dictionary), colour in the second box.

6 How well did you go?

Altimeter
Barometer
Calculator
Clock
Compass
Computer
Dial
Gauge
Hydrometer
Megaphone
Meter
Microphone
Microscope
Odometer
Scales
Seismograph
Spectacles
Speedometer
Stethoscope
Telephone
Telescope
Theodolite
Thermometer
Vane
Watch

0–5   6–10   11–15

16–20   21–25

Colour the activity page, highlighting the award that shows how well you did. Now give your sheet to a classmate to see how many of your words he or she can find.

Name: _____

How many overlocking words can you make?

1 Make a word from the letters in the table, writing it on the board (horizontally or vertically) so that it passes over the star. Cross letters off the table as they are used.

2 Record the points you earn on the pad. You score a bonus 50 points if eight letters are used in one word.

3 If your word passes over a black square, you can triple your word score.

4 Add further words to those already formed as in crossword puzzles, maintaining a progressive score total. A dictionary may be used to check spelling.

5 Play continues until 'time' is called.

WoRd STRetchers

SCRABBLERS ACTIVITY SHEET 1

$A_1 A_1 B_3 C_3 D_2 D_2 E_1 E_1 E_1 F_4 G_2 H_4 I_1 I_1$
$J_8 K_5 L_1 M_3 N_1 N_1 O_1 O_1 P_3 Q_{10} R_1 S_1 S_1 T_1$
$T_1 U_1 U_1 V_4 W_4 X_8 Y_4 Z_{10}$

★			DOUBLE LETTER SCORE			■
DOUBLE LETTER SCORE			DOUBLE LETTER SCORE			
	TRIPLE LETTER SCORE			TRIPLE LETTER SCORE		
		DOUBLE WORD SCORE				
DOUBLE LETTER SCORE			DOUBLE WORD SCORE			DOUBLE LETTER SCORE
	DOUBLE LETTER SCORE			DOUBLE WORD SCORE		
	TRIPLE LETTER SCORE			DOUBLE WORD SCORE		
■		DOUBLE LETTER SCORE			■	

Colour the activity page and give yourself the award you deserve:

- First _____ points
- Second _____ points
- Third _____ points

(Class teacher to set the points for each award.)

Name: _____

How many overlocking words can you make?

1 Make a word from the letters in the table, writing it on the board (horizontally or vertically) so that it passes over the star. Cross letters off the table as they are used.

2 Record the points you earn on the pad. You score a bonus 50 points if eight letters are used in one word.

3 If your word passes over a black square, you can triple your word score.

4 Add further words to those already formed as in crossword puzzles, maintaining a progressive score total. A dictionary may be used to check spelling.

5 Play continues until 'time' is called.

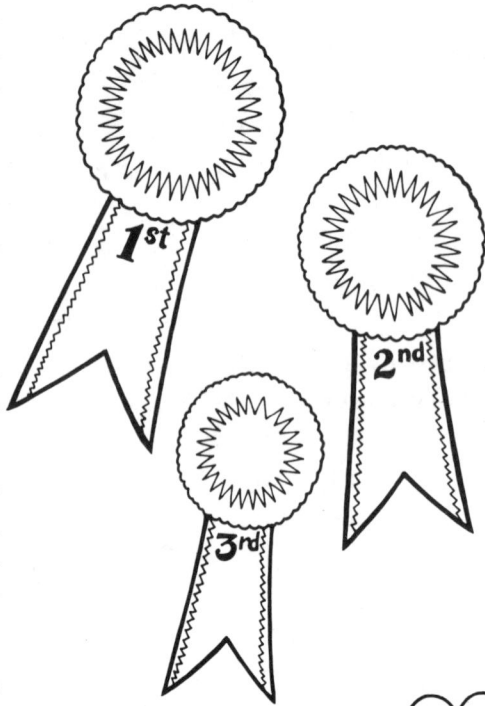

WoRd STRetchers

SCRABBLERS ACTIVITY SHEET 2

$A_1 A_1 B_3 C_3 D_2 D_2 E_1 \ E_1 \ E_1 F_4 G_2 H_4 I_1 \ I_1$

$J_8 K_5 L_1 \ M_3 N_1 N_1 O_1 O_1 P_3 Q_{10} R_1 S_1 S_1 T_1$

$T_1 U_1 U_1 V_4 W_4 X_8 Y_4 Z_{10}$

		DOUBLE LETTER SCORE					★
	DOUBLE LETTER SCORE				DOUBLE LETTER SCORE		
	TRIPLE LETTER SCORE			TRIPLE LETTER SCORE			
			DOUBLE WORD SCORE				
DOUBLE LETTER SCORE		DOUBLE WORD SCORE					DOUBLE LETTER SCORE
	DOUBLE WORD SCORE				DOUBLE LETTER SCORE		
	DOUBLE WORD SCORE			TRIPLE LETTER SCORE			
		DOUBLE LETTER SCORE					

Colour the activity page and give yourself the award you deserve:

- First _____ points
- Second _____ poi
- Third _____ point

(Class teacher to set the points for each award.)

Name: _____

How many overlocking words can you make?

1 Make a word from the letters in the table, writing it on the board (horizontally or vertically) so that it passes over the star. Cross letters off the table as they are used.

2 Record the points you earn on the pad. You score a bonus 50 points if eight letters are used in one word.

3 If your word passes over a black square, you can triple your word score.

4 Add further words to those already formed as in crossword puzzles, maintaining a progressive score total. A dictionary may be used to check spelling.

5 Play continues until 'time' is called.

WoRd STREtchers

SCRABBLERS ACTIVITY SHEET 3

A_1 A_1 A_1 B_3 B_3 C_3 C_3 D_2 D_2 D_2 E_1 E_1 E_1 E_1 F_4 F_4
G_2 H_4 I_1 I_1 I_1 I_1 J_8 K_5 L_1 L_1 M_3 M_3 N_1 N_1 O_1 O_1 O_1
P_3 Q_{10} R_1 R_1 S_1 S_1 T_1 T_1 U_1 U_1 V_4 W_4 W_4 X_8 Y_4 Z_{10}

			DOUBLE LETTER SCORE				
		TRIPLE LETTER SCORE			DOUBLE WORD SCORE		
	DOUBLE LETTER SCORE			DOUBLE WORD SCORE			
DOUBLE LETTER SCORE			DOUBLE WORD SCORE			DOUBLE LETTER SCORE	
		DOUBLE WORD SCORE					
	TRIPLE LETTER SCORE				TRIPLE LETTER SCORE		
	DOUBLE LETTER SCORE			DOUBLE LETTER SCORE			
★			DOUBLE LETTER SCORE				

Colour the activity page and give yourself the award you deserve:

- First _____ points
- Second _____ points
- Third _____ points

(Class teacher to set the points for each award.)

Name: _____

How many overlocking words can you make?

1 Make a word from the letters in the table, writing it on the board (horizontally or vertically) so that it passes over the star. Cross letters off the table as they are used. Space has been provided for you to add extra letters.

2 Record the points you earn on the pad. You score a bonus 50 points if eight letters are used in one word.

3 If your word passes over a black square, you can triple your word score.

4 Add further words to those already formed as in crossword puzzles, maintaining a progressive score total. A dictionary may be used to check spelling.

5 Play continues until 'time' is called.

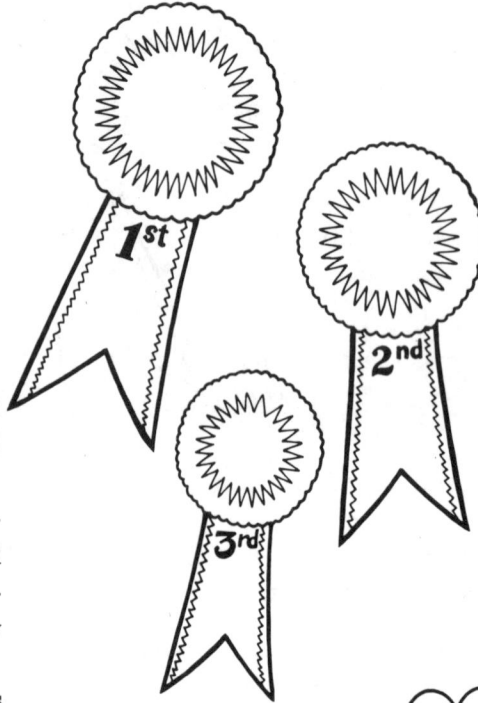

WoRd STRetchers

SCRABBLERS ACTIVITY SHEET 4

$A_1 A_1$	B_3	C_3	D_2	D_2	E_1	E_1	E_1	F_4	G_2	H_4	I_1	I_1
J_8	K_5	L_1	M_3	N_1	N_1	O_1	O_1	P_3	Q_{10}	R_1	S_1	S_1	T_1
T_1	U_1	U_1	V_4	W_4	X_8	Y_4	Z_{10}

★			DOUBLE LETTER SCORE			■
	DOUBLE LETTER SCORE			DOUBLE LETTER SCORE		
		TRIPLE LETTER SCORE			TRIPLE LETTER SCORE	
			DOUBLE WORD SCORE			
DOUBLE LETTER SCORE				DOUBLE WORD SCORE		DOUBLE LETTER SCORE
	DOUBLE LETTER SCORE				DOUBLE WORD SCORE	
		TRIPLE LETTER SCORE				DOUBLE WORD SCORE
■			DOUBLE LETTER SCORE			■

Colour the activity page and give yourself the award you deserve:

- First _____ points
- Second _____ poin
- Third _____ points

(Class teacher to set points for each award.)

Name: _____

Alphabetic Jumbles hide many words. It is just a matter of finding them, for example, STRANGLE and TRAFFIC. Can you find STRAPPING in the example?

Example: An Alphabetic Jumble

Q T R U D F Y I K V Z J E
W S H B A P M C N O X G L

What words of five or more letters can you find in the Alphabetic Jumble below?

1 Look closely at the Alphabetic Jumble and begin searching for hidden words.

2 Words may begin at any letter.

3 The word must be read from left to right, up, down, or diagonally to the right—never backwards (right to left). You may even jump letters.

4 Individual letters may be repeated as long as a backward move isn't made.

5 List any suitable words on the pad.

6 Mark your score (five points per word) on the gauge. How well did you do?

J F M P W N E R Q G Y V Z

B L A O I D T K S H U X C

MY SCORE

Excellent	100
Very, very good	95
Very good indeed	90
Well done	85
Fine effort	80
Satisfactory	75
O.K.	70
Fair	65
Passable	60
Hmmm	55
Well!	50
Could be better	45
Could do a lot better	40
Not good enough	35
Pretty poor	30
Didn't really try	25
Can I try again?	20
Yuk!	15
Shocking	10
Was asleep	5
	0

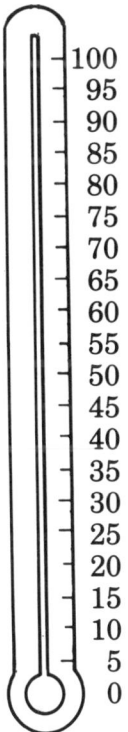

Colour the activity page and show high you were able to score.

Name: _____

Alphabetic Jumbles hide many words. It is just a matter of finding them, for example, STRANGLE and TRAFFIC. Can you find STRAPPING in the example?

Example: An Alphabetic Jumble

Q T R U D F Y I K V Z J E
W S H B A P M C N O X G L

What words of five or more letters can you find in the Alphabetic Jumble below?

1 Look closely at the Alphabetic Jumble and begin searching for hidden words.

2 Words may begin at any letter.

3 The word must be read from left to right, up, down, or diagonally to the right—never backwards (right to left). You may even jump letters.

4 Individual letters may be repeated as long as a backward move isn't made.

5 List any suitable words on the pad.

6 Mark your score (five points per word) on the gauge. How well did you do?

Z C F O U M L A P R G D X

J H Q I K W N S E T B Y V

MY SCORE

Excellent	100
Very, very good	95
Very good indeed	90
Well done	85
Fine effort	80
Satisfactory	75
O.K.	70
Fair	65
Passable	60
Hmmm	55
Well!	50
Could be better	45
Could do a lot better	40
Not good enough	35
Pretty poor	30
Didn't really try	25
Can I try again?	20
Yuk!	15
Shocking	10
Was asleep	5
	0

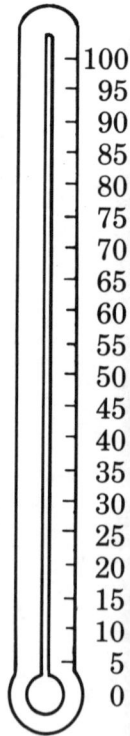

Colour the activity page and show high you were able to score.

Name: _____

Alphabetic Jumbles hide many words. It is just a matter of finding them, for example, STRANGLE and TRAFFIC. Can you find STRAPPING in the example?

Example: An Alphabetic Jumble

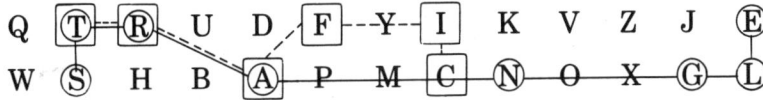

Q T R U D F Y I K V Z J E
W S H B A P M C N O X G L

What words of five or more letters can you find in the Alphabetic Jumble below?

1   Look closely at the Alphabetic Jumble and begin searching for hidden words.

2   Words may begin at any letter.

3   The word must be read from left to right, up, down, or diagonally to the right—never backwards (right to left). You may even jump letters.

4   Individual letters may be repeated as long as a backward move isn't made.

5   List any suitable words on the pad.

6   Mark your score (five points per word) on the gauge. How well did you do?

O P J C W E K Q U G X Z V

M R L A Y B D F I N H T S

MY SCORE

Excellent	100
Very, very good	95
Very good indeed	90
Well done	85
Fine effort	80
Satisfactory	75
O.K.	70
Fair	65
Passable	60
Hmmm	55
Well!	50
Could be better	45
Could do a lot better	40
Not good enough	35
Pretty poor	30
Didn't really try	25
Can I try again?	20
Yuk!	15
Shocking	10
Was asleep	5
	0

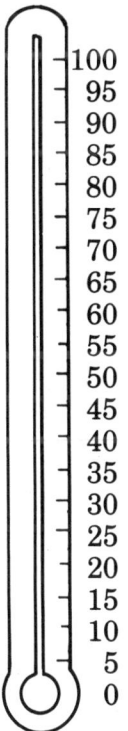

Colour the activity page and show high you were able to score.

59

Name: _____

Alphabetic Jumbles hide many words. It is just a matter of finding them, for example, STRANGLE and TRAFFIC. Can you find STRAPPING in the example?

Example: An Alphabetic Jumble

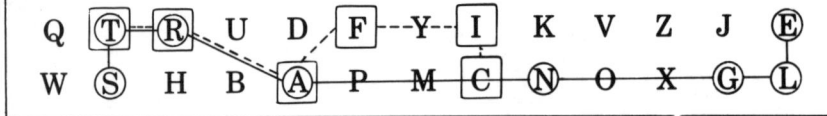

Q T R U D F Y I K V Z J E
W S H B A P M C N O X G L

What words of five or more letters can you find in the Alphabetic Jumble below?

1 Look closely at the Alphabetic Jumble and begin searching for hidden words.

2 Words may begin at any letter.

3 The word must be read from left to right, up, down, or diagonally to the right—never backwards (right to left). You may even jump letters.

4 Individual letters may be repeated as long as a backward move isn't made.

5 List any suitable words on the pad.

6 Mark your score (five points per word) on the gauge. How well did you do?

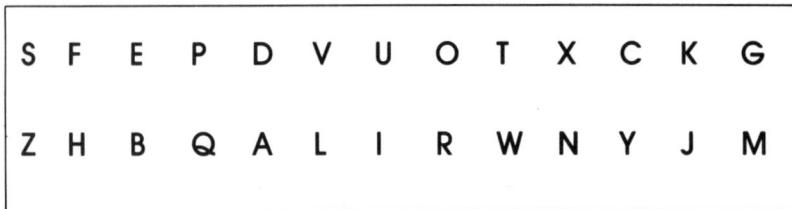

S	F	E	P	D	V	U	O	T	X	C	K	G
Z	H	B	Q	A	L	I	R	W	N	Y	J	M

MY SCORE

Excellent	100
Very, very good	95
Very good indeed	90
Well done	85
Fine effort	80
Satisfactory	75
O.K.	70
Fair	65
Passable	60
Hmmm	55
Well!	50
Could be better	45
Could do a lot better	40
Not good enough	35
Pretty poor	30
Didn't really try	25
Can I try again?	20
Yuk!	15
Shocking	10
Was asleep	5
	0

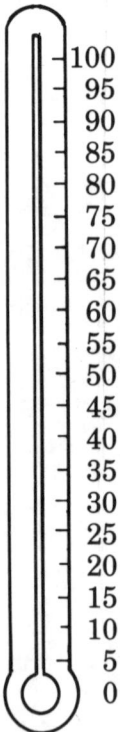

Colour the activity page and show high you were able to score.

Name: _____

Can you find the winning moves?

Can you successfully change a 'starting' word into an 'end' word, in the set number of moves?

1 Change one letter in each word per move.

2 Examples:

- Change HIM to HER in two moves: HIM—HEM—HER

- LOVE can become HATE in three moves: LOVE—HOVE—HAVE—HATE

3 Only real words are permitted. Check your dictionary if in doubt.

4 Various alternatives may be possible.

5 If you can make the changes in fewer moves then you score a bonus of five points.

Now the odds are even!

Go MOOSE

1 H O T   2 C A T   3 B O Y   4 M A T   5 A C E

_____   _____   _____   _____   _____

_____   _____   _____   _____   _____

F A N   D O G   M A N   R U G   O N E

6 WOOD   7 CARD   8 WEEK   9 F OAL   10 S H O E

_____   _____   _____   _____   _____

_____   _____   _____   _____   _____

COAL   GAME   YEAR   COLT   BOOT

11 COOK   12 T A L E

_____   _____

_____   _____   Colour the activity sheet. Total the number of points scored. Don't forget any bonus points and enter your score on the display board.

BOIL   MYTH   Score

Name: _____

Can you find the winning moves?

Can you successfully change a 'starting' word into an 'end' word, in the set number of moves?

1 Change one letter in each word per move.

2 Examples:

• Change HIM to HER in two moves: HIM—HEM—HER

• LOVE can become HATE in three moves: LOVE—HOVE—HAVE—HATE

3 Only real words are permitted. Check your dictionary if in doubt.

4 Various alternatives may be possible.

5 If you can make the changes in fewer moves then you score a bonus of five points.

Now the odds are even!

WoRd STREtchers WINNING MOVES ACTIVITY SHEET 2

₁**FAIR** _____

_____

FOUL

₆**HEAT** _____

_____

COLD

₁₁**FIRE** _____

_____

BURN

₂**SOFT** _____

_____

LOUD

₇**SAIL** _____

_____

SHIP

₁₂**FIND** _____

_____

LOSE

₃**LEAD** _____

_____

GOLD

₈**WARM** _____

_____

COLD

Colour the activity sheet. Total the number of points scored. Don't forget any bonus points and enter your score on the display board.

₄**FROCK** _____

_____

CLOAK

₉**SEEK** _____

_____

FIND

₅**GIVE** _____

_____

TAKE

₁₀**SICK** _____

_____

WELL

Score

Name: _____

Can you find the winning moves?

Can you successfully change a 'starting' word into an 'end' word, in the set number of moves?

1. Change one letter in each word per move.

2. Examples:
- Change HIM to HER in two moves: HIM — HEM — HER
- LOVE can become HATE in three moves: LOVE—HOVE—HAVE—HATE

3. Only real words are permitted. Check your dictionary if in doubt.

4. Various alternatives may be possible.

5. If you can make the changes in fewer moves then you score a bonus of five points.

Now the odds are even!

Go Moose

WORD STREtcHers
WINNING MOVES
ACTIVITY SHEET 3

1 H E R E   2 P A S S   3 C E N T   4 C O L D   5 C O L D

_____ _____ _____ _____ _____

_____ _____ _____ _____ _____

M O O N   F A I L   D I M E   W A R M   H E A T
6 R I S E   7 Z E S T   8 L O S E   9 W E T   10 H A N D

_____ _____ _____ _____ _____

_____ _____ _____ _____ _____

F A L L   L I F E   F I N D
11 W I L D   12 E A S T   D R Y   F O O T

_____ _____

_____ _____   Colour the activity sheet. Total the number of points scored. Don't forget any bonus points and enter your score on the display board.

_____ _____

T A M E   W E S T

Score

Name: _____

Can you find the winning moves?

Can you successfully change a 'starting' word into an 'end' word, in the set number of moves?

1 Change one letter in each word per move.

2 Examples:-

• Change HIM to HER in two moves: HIM—HEM—HER

• LOVE can become HATE in three moves: LOVE—HOVE—HAVE—HATE

3 Only real words are permitted. Check your dictionary if in doubt.

4 Various alternatives may be possible.

5 If you can make the changes in fewer moves then you score a bonus of five points.

WoRd STRetchers WINNING MOVES ACTIVITY SHEET 4

1 DRY	2 SEED	3 WARM	4 MILK	5 READ
___	___	___	___	___
___	___	___	___	___
___	___	___	___	___
WET	TREE	COOL	BOIL	

6 BOAT	7 HILL	8 FLOUR	9 BOOK	BOOK
___	___	___	___	10 HEAD
___	___	___	___	___
___	___	___	___	___
___	___	___	___	___
SHIP	FLAT	BREAD	___	___
			TEXT	FACE

Colour the activity sheet. Total the number of points scored. Don't forget any bonus points and enter your score on the display board.

Score

Name: _____

This pattern will fold into the cube shown below. How many different words can you form from the letters on the cube?

1 Look at the letters on the sides of the cube, and begin searching for words. List the words on the pad.

2 Letters must be read in sequence, with successive letters in a word being located on adjacent sides, for example *may*.

3 Letters may be reused as long as they are in the sequence actually found on the cube.

4 Any word found in a standard dictionary is acceptable. If you are unsure of a word's spelling, check it in your dictionary.

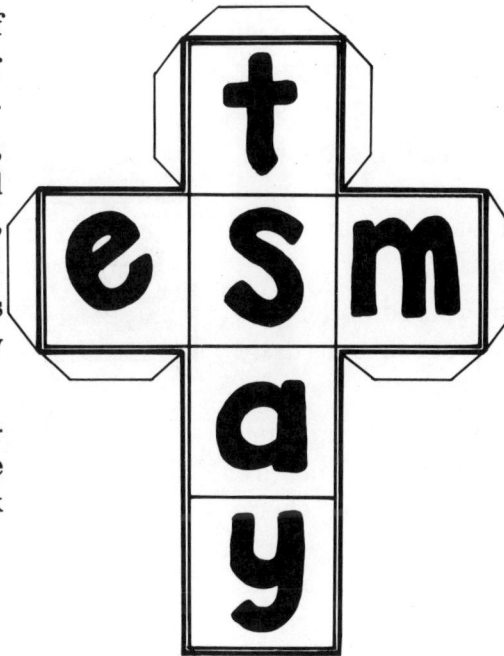

WoRd STRetchers

CUBICS
ACTIVITY
SHEET 1

Colour the activity page and complete the sentence below.

I successfully formed_____**words from the letters on the cube.**

Name: _____

This pattern will fold into the cube shown below. How many different words can you form from the letters on the cube?

1. Look at the letters on the sides of the cube, and begin searching for words. List the words on the pad.

2. Letters must be read in sequence, with successive letters in a word being located on adjacent sides, for example *bird*.

3. Letters may be reused as long as they are in the sequence actually found on the cube.

4. Any word found in a standard dictionary is acceptable. If you are unsure of a word's spelling, check it in your dictionary.

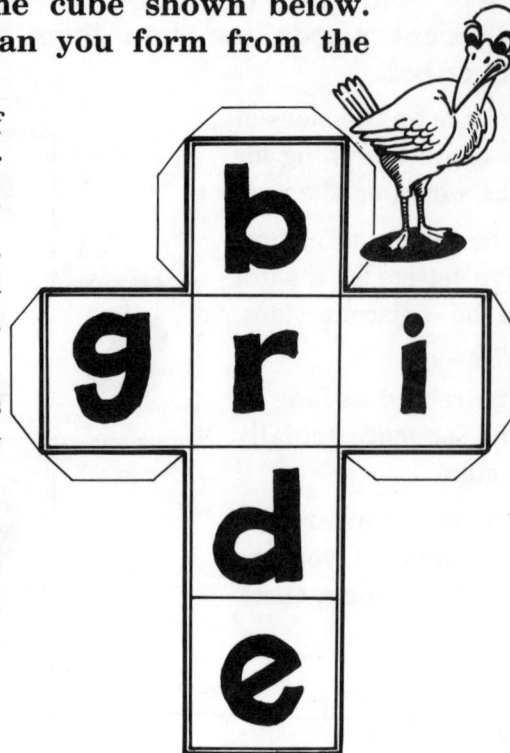

Colour the activity page and complete the sentence below.

I successfully formed_____words from the letters on the cube.

Name: _____

This pattern will fold into the cube shown below. How many different words can you form from the letters on the cube?

1 Look at the letters on the sides of the cube, and begin searching for words. List the words on the pad.

2 Letters must be read in sequence, with successive letters in a word being located on adjacent sides, for example *sky*.

3 Letters may be reused as long as they are in the sequence actually found on the cube.

4 Any word found in a standard dictionary is acceptable. If you are unsure of a word's spelling, check it in your dictionary.

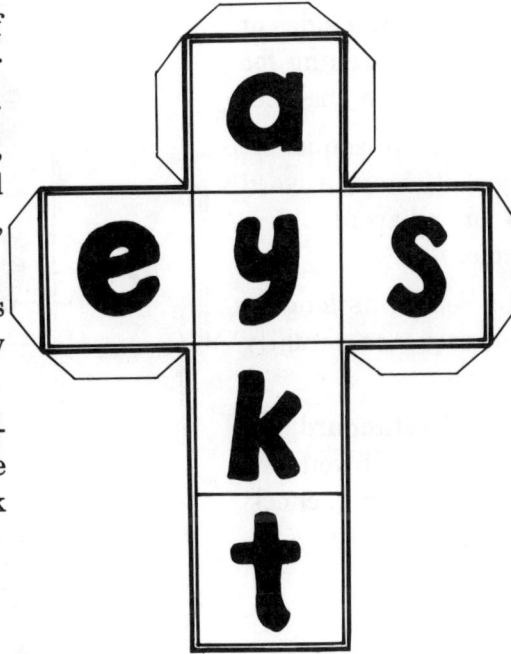

WoRd STRetchers

CUBICS

ACTIVITY SHEET 3

Colour the activity page and complete the sentence below.

I successfully formed_____**words from the letters on the cube.** 67

Name: _____

This pattern will fold into the cube shown below. How many different words can you form from the letters on the cube?

1 Look at the letters on the sides of the cube, and begin searching for words. List the words on the pad.

2 Letters must be read in sequence, with successive letters in a word being located on adjacent sides, for example *now*.

3 Letters may be reused as long as they are in the sequence actually found on the cube.

4 Any word found in a standard dictionary is acceptable. If you are unsure of a word's spelling, check it in your dictionary.

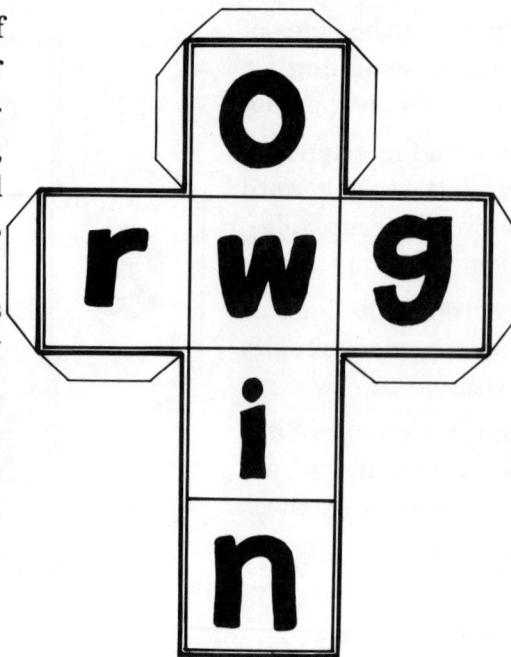

WoRd STREtchers

CUBICS ACTIVITY SHEET 4

Colour the activity page and complete the sentence below.

I successfully formed _____ **words from the letters on the cube.**

Name: _____

How many different words can you make from the letters on this boggler?

1 Look closely at the boggler, searching for words of three letters and more. List the words on the pad.

2 Letters must be read in sequence with successive letters in a word adjoining at a side or corner, for example *fox*. You can't jump letters to make a word.

3 A letter may not be doubled unless it is repeated on the boggler.

4 Only words found in a standard dictionary are acceptable. If you are not sure of a word's spelling, check it in your dictionary.

5 On 'time' count the number of words you have found.

Colour the activity page and give yourself the appropriate award.

- First trophy   15 words
- Second trophy   10 words
- Third trophy   5 words

R	E	N
V	X	F
B	O	T

WoRd STRetChers

BOGGLERS

ACTIVITY SHEET 1

Name: _____

How many different words can you make from the letters on this boggler?

1 Look closely at the boggler, searching for words of three letters and more. List the words on the pad.

2 Letters must be read in sequence with successive letters in a word adjoining at a side or corner, for example *agate*. You can't jump letters to make a word.

3 A letter may not be doubled unless it is repeated on the boggler.

4 Only words found in a standard dictionary are acceptable. If you are not sure of a word's spelling, check it in your dictionary.

5 On 'time' count the number of words you have found.

Colour the activity page and give yourself the appropriate award.

- First trophy   40 words
- Second trophy   30 words
- Third trophy   20 words

M	Y	D
E	A	G
R	E	T

WoRd STRetchers

BOGGLERS

ACTIVITY SHEET 2

Name: _____

How many different words can you make from the letters on this boggler?

1 Look closely at the boggler, searching for words of four letters and more. List the words on the pad.

2 Letters must be read in sequence with successive letters in a word adjoining at a side or corner, for example *barn*. You can't jump letters to make a word.

3 A letter may not be doubled unless it is repeated on the boggler.

4 Only words found in a standard dictionary are acceptable. If you are not sure of a word's spelling, check it in your dictionary.

5 On 'time' count the number of words you have found.

O	U	E	D
A	N	A	D
I	R	A	E
O	U	B	S

WoRd STRetchers

BOGGLERS

ACTIVITY SHEET 3

Colour the activity page and give yourself the appropriate award.

- First trophy — 40 words
- Second trophy — 30 words
- Third trophy — 20 words

Name: _____

How many different words can you make from the letters on this boggler?

1 Look closely at the boggler, searching for words of four letters and more. List the words on the pad.

2 Letters must be read in sequence with successive letters in a word adjoining at a side or corner, for example *beer*. You can't jump letters to make a word.

3 A letter may not be doubled unless it is repeated on the boggler.

4 Only words found in a standard dictionary are acceptable. If you are not sure of a word's spelling, check it in your dictionary.

5 On 'time' count the number of words you have found.

U	I	E	S
E	R	T	Y
B	E	K	N
O	G	I	M

WoRd STRetchers

BOGGLERS

ACTIVITY SHEET 4

Colour the activity page and give yourself the appropriate award.

- First trophy   40 words
- Second trophy   30 words
- Third trophy   20 words

WoRd STRetchers

This *Word Stretchers* activity sheet work-file belongs to:

Name: _____

Year: _____

School: _____

Pupils	ACTIVITY UNITS																															
Class: _____	Unit: Title: Sheet: Date:																															
	1	2	3	4	1	2	3	4	1	2	3	4	1	2	3	4	1	2	3	4	1	2	3	4	1	2	3	4	1	2	3	4

WoRd STRetCheR

CLASS TEACHER'S
PROGRESS
RECORD

Name: _____

Year: _____ Room: __

Teacher: _____

School: _____

Photo/Picture

WoRd STRetchers

PUPIL'S PROGRESS RECORD

L

Well done!
You have satisfactorily completed
_____ *Word Stretchers* units.
You are now entitled to your 'L Plate'.

P

Congratulations!
Because you have finished
_____ units to your
teacher's satisfaction, you have now
earned your 'P Plate'.
(_____ more and you'll have your
Word Stretchers licence).

This is to certify that the bearer
(whose name appears at the top of
this page) is a qualified *Word
Stretcher*, having completed _____ of
the activity units to a satisfactory
standard.

_____   _____
(Class Teacher)   (Date)

This student has continually
achieved excellent standards
throughout the *Word Stretchers*
program.

Honorary Mention

1 Circle Spotters

Activity Sheet 1

he
her
here
red
do
doe
eve
ever
every
very
rye
ye
yea
year
yearn
yearns
ear
earn
earns
a
so
some
somewhere
me
mew
where

Activity Sheet 2

a
at
atop
to
top
pin
pint
pinto
I
in
into
ton
on
no
nor
or
orb
bra
bran
branch
ran
ranch
an
chum

hum
me
meat
eat

Activity Sheet 3

a
all
ally
you
youth
out
has
hasp
as
asp
spin
spine
spines
pi
pin
pine
pines
I
in
nest
the
there
he
her
here
ere
real
really

Activity Sheet 4

self
selfish
elf
elfish
fish
fisher
I
is
she
he
her
hero
row
rowed
owe
owed
we
wed

do
don
done
on
one
net
nether
ether
the
hers
herself

2 'Tis Magic

These are some of the words
that may be created.

Activity Sheet 1

a
am
amber
are
arm
art
at
ate
awe
bar
bare
bat
bate
be
beam
bear
beat
bee
beer
bet
brae
brat
bream
brew
ear
eat
mar
mare
maze
meat
meet
met
mew
rat

raw
raze
tab
tame
tar
tea
team
tear
tee
teem
tram
war
warm
wart
we
wear

Activity Sheet 2

fen
few
foe
foot
he
hen
hew
hose
host
hot
how
nest
net
new

2 'Tis Magic

noose
nose
not
note
of
on
owe
own
sent
set
sew
she
shoe
shone
shot
show
so
soften
son
soon
soot
sow
stew
stow
ten
the
then
those
to
toe
town
we
west
wet
when
who
whose
woe
won

Activity Sheet 3

chide
child
dice
die
dish
he
hid
hide
held
I
is

isle
lie
lied
sex
she
shed
shied
shield
side
six
sled
slid
slide
sly
yes

Activity Sheet 4

a
ape
are
art
at
ate
ear
eat
gap
gate
gave
get
grape
grave
great
gut
hag
have
hear
heart
her
hurt
pare
pat
pave
pea
pear
pert
pure
rag
rage
rape
rapt
rate
rave

rug
rut
tap
tar
the
trap
true
vat

Note: As there are many other possible answers, teacher should check their pupils' work.

3 Keywords

These are some of the words that may be created.

Activity Sheet 1
Apple

a
ale
alp
ape
lap
lea
leap
pal
pale
pap
pea
peal
pep
plea

Pears

a
ape(s)
are
as
asp
ear(s)
pa
par
pare(s)
pea(s)
pear
rap(s)
rape(s)
reap(s)

sap
sea
spar
spare
spear

Peach

a
ace
ache
ape
cap
cape
chap
cheap
each
he
heap
pa
pace
pea

WoRd STRetchers

ANSWERS

Activity Sheet 2

January
a
an
any
aura
jar
jay
jury
nary
nay
ran
ray
run
yarn

August
a
as
at
august
gas
gust
gut(s)
sag
sat
stag
tag(s)
tug(s)
us

March
a
am
arc
arch
arm
car
char
charm
cram
ha
ham
harm
ma
mar
march
ram

Activity Sheet 3

Plastic
a
act(s)
alp(s)
apt
as
asp
at
cap(s)
cast
cat(s)
clap(s)
clasp
is
it
its
lap(s)
last
lip(s)
lisp
list
lit
pact
pat(s)
past
pit(s)
sap
sat
sip
sit
scalp
slap
slip
slit
spat
spilt
spit
splat
split
tap(s)
tip(s)

Silver
I
is
lie(s)
liver(s)
rile(s)
sir
sire
sliver
vie
vile

Copper
cop
cope
core
crop
ore
or
pep
pop
pope
pore
prop
roe
rope

Gold
do
dog
go
god
log
old

Activity Sheet 4

Yellow
lo
low
owe
owl
we
well
woe
ye
yell

Crimson
coin(s)
coir
con(s)
I
in
ion(s)
is
minor(s)
on
or
rim(s)
sin
sir
son

WoRd
STRetChers
ANSWERS

Black
a
cab
la
lab
lack

Purple
lure
pep
per
pup
pure
rule
up

White
he
hew
hi
hit
it
tie
wet
whet
wit

4 Anagrams

Activity Sheet 1

no
own/won
ate, tea
act/cat
arts/rats/tars
step/pest
form
loop/polo
palm
mate/tame/team
pale/peal/plea
knee
lemon
tough
board
pores/spore
acres/cares/scare
reams/smear
bleats/tables
please

Activity Sheet 2

gas
dad
bad
pit
nags/snag
mast
mane/mean
dray
vase
acre/care
part/rapt
once
nerve
taste/teats
slate/steal/tales
salve/slave
lance
bleat
tested
strive

Activity Sheet 3

ten
tub
ape
woe
acne
gulp
ring
tare/tear

lose
diet/edit/tied
lath
ward
strap/traps
teach
large/regal
argon/organ
stone/tones
sweat
stream
tablet

Activity Sheet 4

arc
low
wed
how
sort
stew/wets
rapt/trap
able
shoe
toga
isle
zeal
arts/tsar/star
scent
paste/tapes
grate
leapt/petal/pleat
forest/softer
recipe
resting

5 Step It Out

Teacher to check.

6 Link Letters

Teacher to check.

7 Beat The Barrier

Activity Sheet 1
let

map
hair
milk
tiger
faith
enemy
prince
market
station

Activity Sheet 2

fob
rug
hope
road
apply
relax
pilot
office
person
regular

Activity Sheet 3

paw
age
news
jury
leave
orbit
legal
secret
length
student

Activity Sheet 4

sob
wad
core
idea
chore
motto
debit
search
reward
ancient

Note: Other words may be possible.

WoRd STRetChers ANSWERS

Activity Sheet 1

```
H . G R A N D M O T H E R B
U . . A D O L E S C E N T R
S . . . . . . . . C I . O
B . . . . . . . H E . T
A F F M A N . N . I C T H
N A E . S I S T E R L E E E
D T M M B A B Y P . D . E R
W H A O D A U G H T E R N .
I E L T L M A L E . . A A U
D R E H A S O N W . . D G N
O . . E D I N F A N T U E C
W . . R Y S P O U S E L R L
W I F E . . A U N T . T . E
```

Activity Sheet 2

```
. . . P . L . L . . . . A C
. . . . A . A B O . . . T A
. . . . G S Y U E U . . T R
E N T R Y R S L N D N . I P
C . G V E B E A O D R G C O
S O A N E . A E G B R O E R
P . R R T R . T N E B Y O T
A E A R . O A . H H . Y . M
F B G D I N I N G R O O M .
. . E . D . L D P O U . .
C E L L A R O . E A O O S .
K I T C H E N R . T H R M E
. . V E S T I B U L E . C .
H A L L S H O W E R . . . H
```

Word
Stretchers
ANSWERS

Activity Sheet 3

```
H . W . T R A I N S . S .
E U . I E . . . G . T H .
N . R E N . . N . T O . T
O D L R . D I . S W R . E D
L S R . I N . A E Y M M W R
C . . A T C C R T . P . O I
Y . G H Z R A I W E D T B Z
C O G . E Z D N R . H O N Z
F I E V F I I A E U . D I L
L . O L M W T L N . F A A E
. . O U A U O D B R . N R T
. O H . R G E N O . . R . S
D . . E . R S S . . O . I M
. C L O U D T L I A H T . M
```

Activity Sheet 4

```
C . K O X Y G E N S . . E C
O Y . I . L . S P . T L R
N T D . N U . A . A O E U A
T I . E D T T . . C R K S F
R V . O S E U A . E B C P T
O A M T L I L P H S I O A S
L R G L U T R P S H T R C P
. G I N I A S U M I . . S A
A T H T I O N I S P . H . C
E P U C M D S O E S U . R E
. D O T N S N B R T E A . S
E D A L I U O A T T N R . U
A . O L R A L L U S . P I
. P N . P O E L L . . A .
```

9 Anagralphabets

Activity Sheet 1
state/taste
barn/bran
cent
dare/dear/read
head
farm
angel/angle/glean
hunt
iron
jelly
risk
lamp/palm
mist
brand
notes/stone/tones
dump
quits
tier/tire
dash
tense
suit
dive
wash
oxen
army
zero

Activity Sheet 2
waste
bread/beard
cover
date
frame
first
laugh
hide
onion
jostle
kept
lady
smile/slime
nurse
troop
pilot
quest
drum
seat
tonic
unit
vast/vats
warm
relax
style
zebra

Activity Sheet 3
opera
beard/bread
clear
death/hated
steam/teams/meats
craft
grasp
cheap/peach
noise
joint
knit
bleat/table
medal
novel
groan/organ
person
quits
dream
glass
debt
about
event
water
extra
mayor
laze/zeal

Activity Sheet 4
abate
bleat/table
cheat/teach
desert
tease
forest/foster/softer
logic
other
pupil
jangle
peaks/speak
glare/large
master/stream
nerve/never
oath
spiral
quest
arrest
mares/smear
target
rude
rival
sweat/waste
mixed
yacht
booze

Twenty Words

Activity Sheet 1
architect
butcher
carpenter
dentist
engineer
farmer
glazier
hairdresser
investigator
journalist
lawyer
mechanic
nurse
optician
plumber
reporter
secretary
undertaker
vet
zoologist

Activity Sheet 2
puma
lamb
leopard
gazelle
wolf
orangoutang
cheetah
elk
weasel
ram
lion
kangaroo
asp
alligator
hippopotamus
ferret
gnu
cow
ox
monkey

WoRd STRetchers
ANSWERS

Activity Sheet 3
avocado
rhubarb
garlic
date
cabbage
fig
grape
spinach
broccoli
lettuce
melon
mandarin
mango
parsnip
quince
pear
asparagus
turnip
watermelon
celery

81

10 Twenty Words

Activity Sheet 4

<u>a</u>rchery
<u>b</u>owling
so<u>cc</u>er
gol<u>f</u>
han<u>g</u>-gliding
squa<u>sh</u>
skiin<u>g</u>
cri<u>ck</u>et
bi<u>ll</u>iards
gy<u>m</u>nastics
running
f<u>oo</u>tball
<u>q</u>uoits
<u>r</u>ugby
tenni<u>s</u>
croque<u>t</u>
di<u>v</u>ing
<u>w</u>restling
bo<u>x</u>ing
rugby

Note: Other words may be possible.

11 Cross Grids

Teacher to check.

12 Strip Teasers

Activity Sheet 1
bad
bag
ban
bat
bay
bed
beg
bet
bid
big
bin
bit
bog
boy
cad
can
cat
cod

cog
con
cot
coy
lad
lag
lay
led
leg
let
lit
log
lot
rag
ran
rat
ray
red
rid
rig
rod
rot
sad
sag
sat
set
sin
sit
sod
son

Activity Sheet 2
bald
bale
ball
bead
beat
bell
belt
best
blot
boat
boil
bold
bolt
boot
brag
brat
brig
fail
fall
fast

feat
fell
felt
flag
flat
flit
flog
foal
foil
fold
food
fool
foot
frog
paid
pail
pale
pall
past
pelt
pest
plod
plot
pole
poll
pool
pose
post
prig
prod
tail
tale
teal
teat
tell
test
toad
toil
told
toll
tool
toot
trod
trot
wail
wait
wall
weld
well
welt
west
writ

Activity Sheet 3
ghost
guest
ocean
scant
scare
scarp
scene
scone
scope
score
scorn
scrap
shape
shard
share
sharp
shine
shirt
shone
shore
shorn
short
spare
spend
spent
spine
spore
sport
sprat
sweat

WoRd STREtChers
ANSWERS

12 Strip Teasers

swept
swine
swipe
sword
swore
sworn
there
these
thine
third
thorn
those
twine
twirp
twist
wheat
where
whine
whist
whore
whose

spent
spill
spilt
swank
swear
sweat
sweet
swell
swill
swing
swung
wheat
wheel
whelk
wreak
wring
wrung

Activity Sheet 4

chant
chalk
cheat
cheek
cheer
chill
crank
crawl
creak
creek
crier
cruel
cruet
grant
great
greet
gruel
grunt
oriel
shall
shear
sheer
shell
shunt
spank
speak
spear
spell

13 Hide-and-Seek

Teacher to check.

14 Scrabblers

Teacher to check.

15 Alphabetic Jumbles

These are some of the words that may be found in the alphabetic jumbles.

Activity Sheet 1
blaming
blanks
flaming
flapping
flattery
floods
flowers
joinery
ladder
lowers
madder
manners
mapping
minder

pines
points
ponders
winners
winters

Activity Sheet 2
birth
black
blurry
bonnet
bossy
boxer
dimple
dinosaur
direct
dollar
fixer
goose
march
marry
money
noose
pluck
slack
sleek
slurry
violet

Activity Sheet 3
bedding
fights
laying
moans
moods
mopping
opens
padding
paints
plants
played
plights
praying
rains
reigns
wedding
weeding
weeks
weight
wings

WoRd STRetChers

ANSWERS

Activity Sheet 4
beauty
blink
belong
booty
falling
fellow
flown
halving
hearty
seeping
selling
shallow
sheep
shelling
shirt
shown
slink
sporty
spurt
squirt

Note: As there are many other possible answers, teachers should check their pupils' work.

15 Alphabetic Jumbles

16 Winning Moves

Activity Sheet 1
1 HOT/HAT/FAT/FAN
2 CAT/COT/COG/DOG
3 BOY/BAY/BAN/MAN
4 MAT/RAT/RUT/RUG
5 ACE/ARE/ORE/ONE
6 WOOD/WOOL/COOL/COAL
7 CARD/CARE/CAME/GAME
8 WEEK/WEAK/WEAR/YEAR
9 FOAL/COAL/COAT/COLT
10 SHOE/SHOT/SOOT/BOOT
11 COOK/COOL/COIL/BOIL
12 TALE/MALE/MATE/MYTH

Activity Sheet 2
1 FAIR/FAIL/FOIL/FOUL
2 SOFT/LOFT/LOUT/LOUD
3 LEAD/LOAD/GOAD/GOLD
4 FROCK/FLOCK/CLOCK/
CLOAK
5 GIVE/LIVE/LIKE/LAKE/
TAKE
6 HEAT/HEAD/HELD/HOLD/
COLD
7 SAIL/SAID/SLID/SLIP/SHIP
8 WARM/WARD/CARD/CORD/
COLD
9 SEEK/SEED/SEND/FEND/
FIND
10 SICK/SILK/SILL/SELL/WELL
11 FIRE/FORE/BORE/BORN/
BURN
12 FIND/FINE/LINE/LONE/LOSE

Activity Sheet 3
1 HERE/MERE/MORE/MORN/MOON
2 PASS/PALS/PALL/PAIL/FAIL
3 CENT/DENT/DINT/DINE/DIME
4 COLD/CORD/CARD/WARD/WARM
5 COLD/HOLD/HELD/HEAD/HEAT
6 RISE/RILE/FILE/FILL/FALL
7 ZEST/LEST/LIST/LIFT/LIFE
8 LOSE/LONE/LINE/FINE/FIND
9 WET/MET/MAT/MAY/DAY/DRY
10 HAND/BAND/BOND/FOOD/FOOT
11 WILD/MILD/MILE/MALE/TALE/TAME
12 EAST/FAST/FIST/LIST/LEST/WEST

Activity Sheet 4
1 DRY/DAY/MAY/MAT/MET/WET
2 SEED/SLED/FLED/FREE/TREE
3 WARM/WORM/CORM/CORK/COOK/COOL
4 MILK/MILL/MALL/MAIL/BAIL/BOIL
5 READ/BEAD/BEAT/BELT/BOLT/BOOT/BOOK
6 BOAT/BOAR/SOAR/SOAP/SLAP/SLIP/SHIP
7 HILL/BILL/BELL/BELT/BEAT/FEAT/FLAT
8 FLOUR/FLOOR/FLOOD/BLOOD/BROOD/BROAD/BREAD
9 BOOK/BOOT/LOOT/LOST/POST/PEST/TEST/TEXT
10 HEAD/HELD/HOLD/FOLD/FORD/FORE/FARE/FACE

17 Cubics

These are some of the words
that may be formed from
the letters.

Activity Sheet 1
am
as
east
eyes
mast
may
my
say
seam
set
sty
steam(y)
tea(s)

team(s)
tease
test
yam
yeast
yes
yet

Activity Sheet 2
bed
beg
bib
bid
bide
bed
bribe(d)
bride
bridge

17 Cubics

did
die(d)
edge(d)
grid
rib
rid
ride
ridge

Activity Sheet 3

as
ask(s)
at
ate
east
easy
eat
key(s)
say(s)
stay
taste
tea(s)
yea
yeast
yet

Activity Sheet 4

gig
gin
go
gong
in
no
nor
on
or
rig
ring
row
wig
win
worn
wring
wrong

18 Bogglers

These are some of the words found on the bogglers.

Activity Sheet 1

box
boxer
ere
even
ever
fen
fever
fob
fox
nerve
never
next
oven
over
oxen
vex

Activity Sheet 2

age
are
area
ate
dad
dam
damage
dame
dare
date
day
dye
eager
ear
eat
ere
eye
gad
gadget
gag
gage
game
garage
gate
gay
gear
get
gym
mad
madam
mar
mare
mat

mate
may
meat
meet
mere
rag
rage
ram
rare
rat
rate
ray
read
rear
tag
tame
tamer
tar
tare
tat
tea
team
tear
teat
tee
teem
yam
yea
year

Activity Sheet 3

bane
barb
barn
base
bead
bean
bear
brae
brain
bran
brine
burn
burned
dabs
darn
darned
daub
dead
dean
dear

dene
earn
earned
ease
near
rain
rained
rubs
sadden
sane
sari
sear
sedan
ruin
urine

85

Activity Sheet 4
beet
beget
begin
beret
berth
bets
bogie
ether
eyes
gets
herb
here
hurt(s)
inky
kink
mini
mink
mint(s,y)
oboe
rein
rest
sets
steer
stein
stereo
street(s)
test
tester
tether
thee
there
therein
these
they
three
tree
trek
true

Note: As there may be other possible answers, teachers should check their pupils' work.

WoRd STRetcheR

ANSWERS